Futureproof:

Amplifying Agility with AI and Insightful Business Analysis

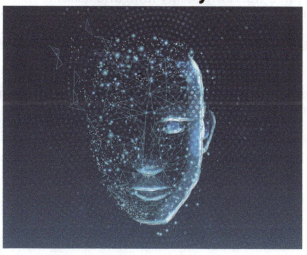

By Angela Wick and Tim Coventry

Published by International Institute of Business Analysis, Toronto, Ontario, Canada.

Print Edition ISBN: 978-1-927584-38-5

eBook Edition ISBN: 978-1-927584-39-2

Any inquiries regarding this publication, requests for usage rights for the material herein, or corrections should be emailed to info@iiba.org.

Preface

The idea for this book was born at the IIBA Building Business Capability Conference in May of 2023. We met in person May 8th, 2023, but, this was not the first time we had "met". We (Tim from Australia, and Angela from the United States) had worked together in a remote/virtual capacity back in 2009 while working on the IIBA Competency Model together. We were used to working together, sharing ideas, and writing together; meeting in person at the conference after 14 years was the inspiration for this book.

In May of 2023 it was 6 months since ChatGPT 3.5 was released and Generative AI showed the world advancements poised to forever change how we work, live, and do business. We had both already been thinking deeply about how Generative AI would change business analysis, the skills needed, the process teams use to develop process and systems changes, and business models. Throughout that week in May, we kept meeting up to talk more and more about it. The idea of this book was born.

As recognized global experts in business analysis practices and competencies, and both having a passion for modernizing analysis practices as technology advances, we both felt a strong pull provide something meaningful to the industry about AI, and NOW.

After getting home from the conference we met each week working on a book outline and goals, and experimented with AI, shared our learnings, and researched the impacts while writing and meeting aggressive deadlines to get this book published with the urgency, we knew it deserved.

AI is poised to change organizations BIG ways! To enable this change, business analysis must adapt in techniques, tasks and skills. From how we participate on software development and business teams, to how we perform our work, and the business models we help our business partners implement; all of these are evolving, making major transformations, impacting the work we do!

The mindset and many key business analysis skills will still be needed. These will need to be elevated and used in new contexts, as well as many new skills to be learned.

Angela Wick

Angela is passionate about modernizing business analysis practices and has over 25 year's of experience doing so! She is the founder of BA-Cube.com, a learning community for business analysis, and a LinkedIn Learning Instructor. Angela's content has been used by over 2 million learners.

Angela has been a BA since the mid 90s and practiced in many industries and on complex projects before becoming a BA Manager in the mid 2000s. In the late 1990s she was put on a project (as a BA Lead) to identify and build a requirements best practice portal for 1000s of analysts. This project sparked a passion for requirements and business analysis work as she interviewed and researched hundreds of teams learning about their practices and what was and was not working and then built out tools, templates, and guides for teams to follow. Since this project, Angela has enjoyed practicing, teaching, mentoring, and continuing to experiment and learn what works for great business analysis outcomes.

She has shared her learnings and knowledge with IIBA and the BA Community globally over the years as a member of the Core Team leading the BABOK v3, Leading the IIBA Competency Model v1, v2, v3, as an item writer on the CBAP exam, and as an expert reviewer on the Agile Extension of the BABOK v3. She has also participated in teams and writings on other business analysis and agile publications as well.

"My passion to promote the value of business analysis and help the community share and build skills is what fuels me, and writing this book with Tim has been a great journey!"

Tim Coventry

 Tim is a seasoned professional with over 30 years of experience in the field of business analysis, currently serving as the CEO of Business Analysis (BAPL) www.business-analysis.com.au, the largest specialist business analysis consultancy in the Southern Hemisphere. BAPL is renowned for offering tailored business analysis services to ASX listed companies, private enterprises, government entities, and not-for-profit organizations. Tim leads BAPL with a commitment to delivering outcome-based services while remaining software and discipline agnostic.

Tim's expertise spans various methodologies, including waterfall, Agile, and product ownership. His practical experience extends from strategic analysis to successful project delivery. He holds a Bachelor of Education and is a Workplace Category IV Trainer and Assessor Certificate holder. Tim is also a distinguished Certified Business Analysis Professional (CBAP), showcasing his dedication to the highest standards in the field.

As an acknowledged expert in business analysis, Tim has made substantial contributions globally. He has presented at prestigious events such as the BA World Symposiums from 2008 to 2011, Building Business Capability in 2013, 2014, and 2023, PMI EMEA Global Congress 2015, PMI Virtual Conference 2016, and the IIBA Australia Chapter BA Professional Day from 2013 to 2023. His international involvement includes working in 18 countries worldwide.

Tim's commitment to advancing the field is evident in his leadership roles. He has served as the President of the IIBA Australia Chapter and has actively participated in International Institute for Business Analysis (IIBA®) forums. Tim is not only an author of the IIBA® Competency Model but also an expert reviewer of the IIBA & Agile Alliance Agile Extension and the IIBA Product Ownership guide.

Outside the professional realm, Tim is a family man, happily married with three children. He balances his busy schedule with a passion for cycling and a love for good wine, often indulging in both pursuits in that particular order.

"My mission in business, NFP and government organizations, is to contribute to the growth and evolution through expertise, leadership, and dedication to excellence in business analysis.

Writing this book with Angela has been a creative, thought provoking and enjoyable journey!"

Dedications

Tim

I dedicate this book to my wife Toni, children Tommy, Sienna & Sierra, Mum & Dad, Uncle Colin & Aunty Lois, Brian & Carol Rogers, Moira McLeod and the BAPL team!.

Angela

I dedicate this book to my family and friends who heard all too often for months "I can't hang out this weekend, I'm working on my book", and I dedicate it to the millions of BAs excited to grow, learn, and lean into this new era of business analysis.

Table of Contents

Preface i

Introduction 1

Chapter 1: Business Analysis—The Beginning Starts NOW! 5

  The Next Phase 7

  What Needs to Change to Keep Up 11

  Chapter Summary 20

  Action Items 20

Chapter 2: What Good, Bad, and Ugly Analysis
            Looks Like—Before and with AI............................. 21

  Current State: Most Organizations are Doing Poor or
  Average Analysis—and it is Costing Them! 22

  An Analysis Framework for a New Era 37

  Risks of Not Upping the Analysis Game......................... 42

  Leveraging AI Through Insightful Business Analysis 43

  Chapter Summary 45

  Action Items 45

Chapter 3: Understand the Past in Order to Navigate the Future 47

How Did We Get Here? 48

AI Analysis Accelerator Framework—Accelerating
Continuous Value in an AI World 57

The Skills Gap and the Urgency to Upskill 59

Thriving Organizations 60

Chapter Summary 60

Action Items 61

Chapter 4: Future State—Analysis is NOT a Phase! 63

Continuous Improvement and Analysis is Intuitive 64

Continuous Improvement—Continuous Analysis 65

The AI Analysis Accelerator Framework and
How the Concepts Fit Together 76

Paradigm Shifts for Continuous Analysis 78

Chapter Summary 83

Action Items 83

Chapter 5: Business Analysis Roles in the Future 85

The Future Business Analyst 86

Business Analysis is "Knowledge Work" 86

A Larger Ecosystem—Back to our Example 87

Knowledge Work Enables Strategic Alignment Facilitation 91

Facilitate Constant Prioritization 97

Business Analysis in the Future 98

Chapter Summary 103

Action Items 103

Chapter 6:   Implications of AI on Business Analysis 105

Adapting to an AI-Dominated Future:
The Evolving Skillset 106
Productivity 108
SDLC and Team Collaboration Changes 113
New Business Models 117
New Skills and Focus for Business Analysts
that will Evolve with AI 118
Chapter Summary 118
Action Items 119

Chapter 7:   Future Skills and Competency 121

Leveling Up 122
The Speed of Skill Development in an AI-Driven World 135
Cultural and Global Changes 137
Chapter Summary 138
Action Items 138

Chapter 8:   Setting Up Business Analysts for Success 139

Setting the Path to Success 141
An Updated View of Business Analysis 148
Chapter Summary 149
Action Items 149

Chapter 9:   How to Build These Competencies 151

Building Competency is a Continuous Journey 152
What Does Building Competency Mean? 154
Factors Influencing Competency Development 160
What to Focus on First—A Roadmap to Get There 161
Chapter Summary 171
Action Items 172

Chapter 10: Last Words from Samantha Ghent 173

Introduction

In our rapidly changing world of technological and artificial intelligence (AI) advancements, the demand for organizations to undergo metamorphic transformations is increasing. Their success, and, in many cases, their survival will rest on their ability to adapt, pivot, and respond to the speed and complexity they face. Business analysis will be a critical competency in an organization's ability to keep up.

Harmonizing human knowledge with AI-augmented analysis will be a key practice for organizations to adopt. Organizations must quickly learn how to implement innovations that used to take months to deliver. Continuous business analysis is the critical path to enable this by understanding the big picture and specific details of how value is delivered.

This book unravels the direct correlation between good business analysis, business agility, and AI. Organizations require good business analysis to survive as AI and other technological advances accelerate complexity. We are at the junction of revolutionary change, and it is already clear that good business analysis is not merely a nice to have, but is mandatory for innovation and strategic change.

In this book we dive into the key themes that will unlock what DNA organizations require for high-performing business analysis. We will guide the leaders and practitioners who perform and lead business analysis in their organizations on how to navigate the changing practices and mindsets needed for success.

The impact of AI on organizations will be deeply profound, wide reaching, and, in some cases, catastrophic. To be an AI-first organization, many existing practices will no longer serve teams in delivering value at the pace needed. Business analysis practices that are entrenched in software delivery processes, where the focus is on performing requirements elicitation from stakeholders, managing backlogs, writing user stories, and defining specs for solutions, will no longer serve organizations in being competitive or cost effective.

In an AI-immersed world, business analysis is the catalyst between strategy and organizational change. In this book we advocate that high-level analysis that is well connected to the details will be paramount. That is, analysis focused on the customer, users, and value-rather than the technology-will drive AI solution success. The direct connection between customers, users, strategy, products, systems, and features has always been a key to success, yet the skill to align these components has been lacking. AI advancements are creating a pace of change and delivery that makes it imperative to understand higher-level organizational connections in order to deliver meaningful solutions.

Business analysis will guide the implementation, integration, and continuous improvement of AI solutions within organizations. This involves the reuse of analysis **assets**, not recreating them for every project and initiative. Asset reuse enables the value, speed, and quality of AI solutions, and this will be explored throughout the book.

Within this world infused with AI, organizations need a new path to work efficiently to deliver strategic change. No longer will organizations survive with large project failures or endless backlog prioritization. Throughout this book, we will introduce a framework for business analysis that will enable strategy and AI to thrive in alignment with one another. Utilizing the power and efficiency of AI, our framework, will

- connect the analysis to strategy and delivery,

- proactively leverage data analytics for evidence-based decision-making on priorities and what to focus on next,

- allow the continuous use of **assets** that can be used for analysis, created jointly by AI and humans, which are normally developed from scratch for every new initiative, or previously have been too expensive to maintain,

- enable continuous improvement using **hypotheses and experiments** to reduce risks and increase learning velocity, and

- enable continuous connection and alignment of the **team tasks and activities** that teams undertake to align to the strategic intent.

History has proven how difficult delivering value can be, and many organizations struggle to plan, deliver, and measure project value. Our framework concentrates prioritization on measurable results. Every organization should be focused on the customer and **user behavior changes** that drive business value. Cultivating a culture of measuring, evaluating, and influencing positive customer and user behavior is a must. Business analysis is the cornerstone of tracing these metrics to realize organizational improvements and strategic intent.

Another drastic change for business analysis in the new era of AI is the increased usage of data analytics (descriptive, diagnostic, predictive, and prescriptive) to drive speed and agility. Real-time data analytics will enable user behavior changes to be monitored, closely tracking incremental changes. These instantaneous data analytics enable organizations to continuously monitor user behavior changes. Even small changes in behavior patterns will be noticeable, and subtle implementation changes can be made that may have been impossible previously.

Predictive analytics help us more quickly assess what the potential user behavior trends and patterns are likely to be over time. This enables us to build solutions that respond to trends more quickly. Improved data analytics will enable practitioners to understand the meaning of spikes, drops, and peaks in the user behavior. This gives teams and leaders a clearer view, helping to more quickly determine the action needed to produce desired outcomes.

Business analysis competencies and skills require a seismic shift to embrace the full potential of AI. A higher level of competency in many common business analysis skills will be needed to leverage AI and strategic alignment. Continuous learning is key to developing these competencies and skills across many roles in the organization. The biggest lift will come from centering skill learning on the metrics and measurement of an organization's success.

Alignment from strategic intent to the work details will help continuously realize the organizational strategy.

We cannot predict how quickly AI will be implemented to change business models or software development processes across organizations; however, we can see that the transition has started. Our vignettes that we begin each chapter with are fictional representations of what the future of analysis within AI-first organizations might look like. Organizations can unlock the full potential of AI when a cultural change occurs in how business analysis is seen, practiced, and leveraged.

So, let's dive into how you can gain valuable insights into leveraging good business analysis now and into the future.

1 Business Analysis—The Beginning Starts NOW!

In this chapter we lay out the context of business analysis in initiatives, projects, business change, technology change, and artificial intelligence; and where they are heading.

We discuss the massive and exponential changes happening that are influencing needed changes in how we work and why business analysis is critical to these changes.

We begin to lay out how AI implementations in organizations will need to leverage business analysis and an elevated approach to business analysis to survive and thrive.

Vignette

Samantha Ghent

My eyes squint as I try to make out the blurry numbers on my phone, 4:13am, or is it 4:31? No matter what the time, I do not want to be awake at this hour on a Sunday morning.

I don't want to wake my partner either, so I quietly grab my glasses to see what the alert is about. As my eyes come into focus, I can tell it is an alert from work; a system component has lost connection and until it is fixed it is losing the company $220,260 per hour.

Now I am awake!

Before I get myself too worked up, a few minutes later I get another alert that the connection has been reestablished based on a variable being updated in the code. Automated testing has already passed all test cases, and transactions are successfully being processed again.

Whew!

My name is Samantha Ghent, and I am the CTO/CIO of a large organization that is fully leveraging AI and business analysis.

I have had this vision for years—although maybe we will call it a dream—a dream where I would understand the cost impact to the organization of a single (technical) piece in the value stream not working.

In fact, this capability has been around forever, but the cost to plan, analyze, and implement this has always been too high. As AI has changed how we work, this vision has become far less expensive and troublesome to implement, and we are there! We have implemented process automations like

- *AI generating code,*
- *AI automating testing,*
- *mapping and linking our customer journeys and value streams to the code, so our software exactly follows our process,*
- *linking our customer journeys and value streams to data analytics for each business and user process,*
- *predicting, writing, modeling, and assigning the code that needs to be updated, in an automated test environment, before assigning a risk value, and then automatically deploying when certain thresholds and conditions are met,*
- *creating workflows to alert the right leaders about the severity of issues based on an analysis model of how much money the issue is costing us, and*
- *being an AI-first, data-and evidence-driven organization leveraging business analysis in combination with AI to plan, analyze, predict, model, and manage our business processes.*

The key to all of this?

Good business analysis.

AI alone does not add value; good analysis linking the value stream, data, and SDLC to AI is valuable, oh so valuable!

My story will continue throughout the book.

The Next Phase

Business analysis is critical to organizations and will be even more so in the next phase of how organizations survive and thrive in an AI-driven world.

As we move to this next phase of artificial intelligence (hereafter, AI) and automation, only those organizations that innovate and shape the future will last. We have seen it for decades now—the lifespan of organizations is shrinking. The survivors will be those that innovate. Usability of software, customer satisfaction, and customer experience will continue to have higher and higher expectations.

In order to survive and thrive, organizations will need to use business analysis to

- balance the use of human and AI intelligence in the analysis, innovation, and development processes,

- use sound judgment in implementing AI into business models and processes with a focus on value, and

- enable continuous improvement, focused on improving the customer and internal business users' experience.

> A recent study by McKinsey found that the average lifespan of companies listed in Standard & Poor's 500 was 61 years in 1958. Today, it is less than 18 years. McKinsey believes that, in 2027, 75% of the companies currently quoted on the S&P 500 will have disappeared.
>
> They will be bought-out, merged, or will go bankrupt like Enron and Lehman Brothers. Some companies manage to escape this mass destruction. General Electric, Exxon Mobile, Procter &Gamble and DuPont are among the oldest companies on the New York Stock Exchange.Nevertheless, the largest market capitalizations today have new names: Apple, Alphabet, Microsoft, or Amazon."[1]

Organizations that continuously improve the customer experience in this way will survive the threat of competitors and retain their market share across the globe. The key differentiators for organizations in the future will be

- the speed and pace at which they can improve their product and service offerings and take market share away from their competitors,

1. https://www.imd.org/research-knowledge/disruption/articles/why-you-will-probably-live-longer-than-most-big-companies/
#:~:text=A%20recent%20study%20by%20McKinsey,S%26P%20500%20will%20have%20disappeared

- how they leverage AI to monitor where processes are compromised and recommend solutions (AI will predict the issues and opportunities before we realize they even are issues and opportunities; it will be up to our business analysis capabilities to drive and facilitate these AI-driven recommendations), and

- how they develop processes and systems that make human actions easy for internal and external users and customers.

Business analysis has been critical to helping organizations thrive over the past 20 years and will become more so as we move to more dynamic, responsive, AI-first organizations.

This book sets out to show how by aligning organizations' strategic directives to impactful metrics, and then to the value streams and insights from predictive and prescriptive analytics, organizations will have a stronghold on innovation, customer demand, and cost efficiencies.

Elements of the next phase and future of business analysis are being driven by forces outside of our control. These forces must not be ignored, but rather taken into account as we adapt our practices, processes, and skills in how we perform and enable business analysis within small, medium, and large organizations.

We are not looking to throw out any other frameworks or methodologies; rather, this book helps those performing business analysis and organizations connect them through powerful business analysis. We are calling for a way of doing business analysis that is strategic, yet practical, that is both **business results** and customer obsessed, and that weaves aspects of process, technology, data, systems, people, and AI together into a continuous improvement approach that enables AI and agility.

Let's look at the factors that will help these organizations get there through AI and business analysis.

Context Influencing the Future of Business Analysis

The factors influencing the need for analysis practices to adapt and level up include

- an increased pressure for a fast product to market launch,

- global markets requiring a rapid response to compliance (local and global), and

- high personal customization of products and services.

Increased Pressure for a Fast Product to Market Launch

Product launch speed and pace are directly related to the analysis that is performed. Exceptional business analysis can and should be done continuously as teams build and monitor the performance of the business and user processes. This goes beyond an analysis phase, but rather a need for continuous analysis.

Good analysis enables organizations to accelerate pace and speed through the use of data, and customer empathy. Understanding what customers actually need and how it aligns to organizational strategy is paramount to fast and relevant delivery. Teams utilizing **assets**, data, and predictive and prescriptive analysis will be able to deliver faster and with better quality. The accuracy of this analysis will therefore be key to making sure that the product is on point, to allow precise delivery that is on target quickly and accurately.

Organizations that maximize their **assets** with AI will be able to trial new features and new offerings much quicker than competitors, be more cost efficient, respond to market changes faster, and cut off projects that are not aligning, to deliver results. Customers will be more likely to take up the new offerings that the speed and customization of the continual improvement of the products and services provide.

Global Markets: Rapid Response to Compliance (Local and Global)

As we shift further toward a global economy, compliance for organizations will also become more global. There will be more and more large scale changes that will cause disruptions for organizations, big and small, such as the General Data Protection Regulation (GDPR), which disrupted many global companies.

Compliance is often scattered across multiple value streams, customer journeys, and systems, which causes major delays in responding to change. In the future, organizations with silo-structured business units—with restricted software and systems that only deliver a portion of the value stream—will struggle to make fast, effective compliance changes.

Organizations structured on value streams aligned to AI, however, will be dynamic in identifying required changes and be able to apply new configuration with speed unlike what we have seen in the past.

High Personal Customization to Products and Services

Pre-Industrial Revolution, personalization was king, as those who made products, made them personally for each customer; they owned their craft! If you wanted a suit, it was planned, built, and tailored to your size and preferences, made specifically for you. Then, with the Industrial Revolution, efficiency, mass production, and cost became the business drivers to compete, which often left personalization out of reach for many as the cost basis was so much higher.

Since the digital era and AI have taken hold, we are swinging back to more personalization in all industries, while using AI to bring cost efficiencies and value at scale. The pace of change will continue its exponential curve in advancements, and we will see many changes to organizations around the world. We will witness companies offering more divergent products and services with ever-greater consumer personalization. Let us look at some examples.

The manufacturing industry has been and will continue to change dramatically. The car industry, for example, over the last decades has become a much more flexible and tailored industry. Robotics has enabled the sale of custom, configurable items. Gone are the days of Henry Ford, who produced automobiles that you could choose "any color as long as it was black." Now, millions of configurations are available with a click of a mouse, and the production process is automated to handle this. Generative AI (GenAI) brings another angle to this as the robots used to create automobiles (and all sorts of manufactured products) can leverage software-driven, customizable tooling, increased data analytics, and GenAI.

Transportation is also becoming safer, easier, and more convenient than ever before with greater flexibility from autonomous self-driving vehicles, planes, trains, trucks, and ships. Yes, we have already seen this in the works for decades, yet the latest advancements will only make the accuracy, quality, and speed to deliver these changes faster!

The software industry has exploded with the number of personalized software systems that are available in the marketplace. As AI increasingly becomes a larger part of these, we will continue to see more customization and personalization that will amaze us. Software is and will better predict what we are trying to accomplish and make us much faster at everyday tasks.

Banking and fintech are increasingly leveraging AI and data, from predicting our needs to managing and predicting portfolios, as well as fraud detection. This makes everyone's role in each of these processes far more efficient.

The fast-food industry has seen many changes, including delivery of food from kitchen to household door. AI will continue to evolve this in the customer service areas, as well as in the supply chain, kitchen/ingredient storage, delivery, and order management.

The fishing industry has also changed, through the use of software that records catches and species, and through tagging fish to provide better management of the resources within the oceans. Fish-locating software will increasingly improve the accuracy of locating, fishing, and processing specific species. Knowing more about specific species could also help the reduction of over-fishing.

Health care is a major area that is leveraging AI, and we will see significant advances here. Using large language models (LLM) and deep learning, the speed to detect, diagnose, and treat disease is accelerating dramatically. The speed to produce new medications and treatments is already showing amazing advancements with AI.

Customers increasingly expect and can have personalized experiences, products, and services, and it is easier than ever to leave one provider to get what we want from another. Therefore, organizations that continue to focus on cost efficiencies over customer experience, and traditional technologies over AI, will lose the cost battle to those that are focusing on AI for a better customer and user experience for both internal and external users and customers.

> Yes, we must be cost efficient, but cost efficient through value analysis. Value analysis that minimizes the work done while maximizing the value delivered.

The pace of change will continue its exponential curve in advancements, and we will see many changes to organizations around the world. We will witness companies offering more divergent products and services with ever-greater consumer personalization.

What Needs to Change to Keep Up

In subsequent chapters we will look at how business analysis will need to change to keep up with the future context and thrive. We will explore themes like the following, which we have introduced next:

- Monitoring processes proactively

- Business analysts facilitating citizen development

- Responsive customer feedback

- A rapid-learning work force for innovation—skills first

Monitoring Processes Proactively

Today, many business analysis efforts are centered around requirements elicitation, or as some call it, "requirements gathering." Various techniques are used to research, collaborate, and discuss requirements with business leaders and users. Together, they identify what needs to be done to improve the business process, user performance, and systems.

In an AI-enabled organization we are able to continuously monitor user and business processes with greater ease, speed, accuracy, and at less cost than before. This will allow us to be far more proactive in discovering issues and opportunities long before a business stakeholder or customer reports them. Imagine the items you work on are based data that shows how bad a problem actually is. Imagine having increased feasibility in modeling how well different options might perform given recent organizational and customer performance.

Good analysis enables organizations to define and measure value streams and customer journeys. If these are well defined, they can easily be linked to strategic imperatives as well as system details. Meaningful measurements, monitored with data analytics, are defined and aligned to strategic OKRs, and KPIs; creating measurements linking the strategic intent to the details.

Business analysts are primed to be value-stream monitors; evaluating the strategic alignment, risk, operations performance, and customer journeys, and how system details are improving or hindering success.

> Focus on learning, unlearning, and relearning—continuous learning that maps strategic imperatives to value streams, to system and user processes, and maps data to these to enable AI to leverage data insights for strategy.

Measured value streams and AI can leverage data analytics to track immense amounts of data and see patterns in how users and customers are behaving with their actions and processes.

Leveraging data analytics with well-defined value streams can alert leaders and analysts to where processes are not performing and can be improved. AI is poised to suggest whether current compliance or product features are suboptimal, and then model potential fixes to the issues. This can all happen faster than most leaders even know there is a problem.

Setting up an analysis ecosystem that monitors business and customer processes is a game-changer. Monitoring business and customer processes isn't a new capability; what is new is how much AI can help get this type of ecosystem set up, as long as the strong analysis skills are present to define, set up, and keep it up to date.

With this, imagine a business analyst, for example, monitoring a suite of value streams, taking on 10x–100x more work than previously. Business analysis can fully leverage AI to help understand where the issues are, what is most impacting business performance, and what changes are most impactful. Good business analysis practices will create more strategic alignment using evidence-based data to prioritize and facilitate the findings and decisions with business and tech leaders.

We will face challenges along the way, such as data quality, quality control, data ownership, data privacy, and bias. Understanding what AI can do and how to partition the data (internal and external data sources) for users and processes, based on need, will also be a challenge. Business analysts will be part of solving these issues. For example, by deciding what data is used in internal LLMs as knowledge; evaluating the data quality and risks of using the data for what uses; as well as what user groups should have access to what knowledge and data when using AI in their work, and for what scenarios.

Business Analysts Facilitate Citizen Development

For several years, many organizations have been experimenting with "low code" and "no code" development. Things like robotic process automation (RPA), service-oriented architectures, rules engines, and the like have been around for many years now.

With GenAI, another level of no and low code is possible. GenAI is enabling no and low code solution development at a greater scale than before, with the cycle and process to design, build, test, and deploy solutions changing, often from months to a single day.

"Citizen development" is the concept of non-software engineers—i.e., everyday employees—being able to use GenAI tools with plain language prompting or an interface to a GenAI agent, to create applications, update applications, and make production changes. These efforts need really good business analysis to deliver the right value.

As GenAI continues to grow in its usage, and especially for automating code, reusing code, and writing code, the critical path is no longer the programming. The analysis to define and create the solution, covering all the needed user scenarios, becomes the critical path. Analysis includes the work needed to deeply understand the users, user groups, goals, actions, scenarios, rules, exceptions, triggers, and the various data variances that can happen. AI can also help make this work more efficient. Business analysts are using AI in harmony with their knowledge and analysis skills to get the work done much faster. Without this analysis, many no and low code apps can be built, but the value they actually add will be quite questionable and could ultimately result in a lot of rework, painful workarounds, and waste.

Citizen development with good analysis—paired with strong IT governance to ensure stable data, performance, and security—has a lot of promise. It has the potential to bring immense changes and efficiencies to organizations. When used well, it can lessen the struggle between IT and business/user groups. When used incorrectly, however, it can bring disaster and an organization to its knees!

The answer lies along a spectrum of risk. Systems, processes, and value streams have varying complexities. No matter how complex a system is, there is an opportunity for some pieces to enable citizen development.

How does an organization decide what is appropriate for citizen development? Careful business analysis! It's an analysis of the interactions between user actions, data, and rules. Also looking at the data and cyber security risks. Where these are very straightforward, and changes to pieces of this can be contained with boundaries and automated testing, it's definitely possible.

Imagine a business manager of a pricing department being able to configure and create a new product category and pricing structure on their own, without an IT support request and a six-to twelve-month project. Or a healthcare organization being able to change the workflow of how patients are communicated to in hours or days, rather than months.

The concept of business teams and users making changes on their own is intriguing. Business analysis is needed to help determine the risk of each user group and actions. This would entail establishing a risk profile and boundaries of what rules and data can be changed, updated, added, or removed, and then automatically tested without risking the process and value stream. Business analysis would also help in the building of an automated test case suite that would be run before any change is deployed.

These business users will no doubt need skills to do this. Many will be business analysis skills and many will be business analysts! After all, what business team has the resources idly sitting around with the time to do this work?

In the concept of teams using a business analyst to make the changes for them, these professionals will need to

- facilitate what ideas/changes will add the most value,

- facilitate the decisions on the implementation details and the details that impact each user group's workflow,

- connect and analyze users, goals, processes, data, and rules to value streams and strategy,

- analyze and elicit the scenarios with the user groups,

- configure/prompt for the application's function, rules, features in a test environment using GenAI,

- identify more complex test case scenarios, and have the skills to configure the automation of these scenarios,

- connect with a larger IT suite of systems and integrations to test downstream impact, and

- connect with larger IT infrastructure and governance processes.

In the case of highly complex changes, a business analyst will need to

- define and communicate the strategic intent and metrics that will measure success, as well as the existing value stream,

- facilitate conflicting stakeholder needs to decisions that maximize strategic intent, while satisfying all stakeholders,

- implement monitoring measurements as the team builds,

- analyze and elicit the scenarios with the user groups and connect to larger value streams across the organization,

- work with a development team that uses GenAI and prebuilt functions to configure/prompt for the new functions, rules, features in a test environment using GenAI,

- experiment and run prototypes,

- identify more complex test-case scenarios, and have the skills to configure the automation of these scenarios,

- connect with a larger IT suite of systems and integrations to test downstream impact, and

- connect with larger IT infrastructure and governance processes.

There will also be significant work in many organizations to set up and define the citizen development environments and boundaries for the business users. This needs business analysis as well!

All of these requisites will require a completely different way of working. One with a much more collaborative end-to-end and continuous learning culture, to keep up with the constant change.

Without a massive investment in business analysis capabilities, citizen development at any level can easily go awry. Organizations will need to develop critical-thinking and analysis skills of how automations use and transform data. They will also need to develop real business measurements that need to be in place to monitor and test that things are working as intended. Coming up with the test cases, scenarios, and data to run them appropriately is a complex analysis task.

Responsive Customer Feedback

Customer feedback has always been difficult to gather, interpret, and act on. Teams are often pressured to move forward with business leaders' ideas, rather than evidence-based and meaningful customer feedback at scale. In an AI-first world, leveraging data and the power of AI, along with interpreting and acting on customer feedback, can be faster and further amplified. We can more easily see patterns in data, ask an AI agent to interpret data for us, explore predictions, and model prescriptive ideas. We can more easily set up, use, and leverage evidence-based data to make decisions among teams and stakeholders. Not leveraging these capabilities will cost organizations deeply.

We can be so much more in touch with what users are experiencing when using our products and services. We need to adopt a mindset, culture, and skillset in the organization that enables us to leverage more data to understand the user experience. Now, AI will help us get there faster and with less cost and effort.

Setting up and leveraging data analytics and AI to ignite the power of customer and user feedback insights and analytics will be a powerful tool that we will look at in subsequent chapters.

Rapid-Learning Workforce for Innovation: Skills First

Upskilling, reskilling, and shifting skills across the organization is clearly an imperative in today's organizations. Business analysis skills are no different. Organizations will not only need to upskill business analysis professionals, but also build analysis skills throughout the organization in other roles as well. Analysis professionals that are skilled at high levels will be able to bring out elevated analysis in other roles.

Making this mindset happen in organizations is not a small effort. Upskilling employee knowledge to leverage AI and the data, and then be consultative in connecting the work to the organizational strategy and metrics, sounds downright dreamy and scary.

It's one thing to understand AI technically, but it's another to understand the business and ethical applications of it. This involves understanding it at various levels of context as well as its detailed application within business processes, value streams, and customer journeys. We can't just "implement AI everywhere." Strong analysis must be done to determine many of the details of implementation and usage of AI so that it actually makes the difference we intend it to make, without concurrent negative impact.

It's one thing to have business knowledge, but it's another to understand how this business knowledge can be broken down and analyzed in terms of the connections between value, users, actions, customer journeys, workflows, data, and rules.

It's one thing to understand the organization's strategy and measurements, but it's another to connect them tightly to every action a customer takes, or an internal employee takes, and be able to measure each step's effectiveness and alignment with strategic goals.

It's one thing to see the data on how a process performed last month, but it's another to get a real-time alert when the process is deviating from a norm, with recommendations on the cause and possible solutions.

It's one thing to guess at what requirements might create a needed business and customer behavior change to increase sales or decrease costs, but it's a game-changer to be able to model a change against a chosen set of production data and see how it performs before implementing it.

Now, add on the skills to analyze customer journeys, systems workflow, a new model of software development leveraging GenAI, new roles, new power structures, and new communications structures in the organization, and you have a crazy amount of change happening at once.

Impossible? Yes, if organizations refuse to relearn their business unit ownership, roles, and decision processes. Organizations structured in traditional silos will not be competitive. These organizations will work at a snail's pace compared to others.

But it is not impossible for those organizations aligning to do end-to-end analysis, connecting the strategic intent to the details. This is what is needed to thrive into the next decade and make changes at a pace unheard of a few years ago.

In later chapters we discuss the skills and techniques needed to succeed in the call for higher-level analysis in more detail, as well as the path to grow them in yourself or your team/organization.

Out pace Competitors … or Die

Organizations and individual analysis practitioners that understand AI can reimagine how they interact with customers and deliver value; harnessing AI's benefits to enable their organizations to outpace the competition.

These organizations will

- identify the most important things of value to work on faster than others,

- **experiment** and model possible solutions before others can even identify the problem, and

- implement and measure changes to be confident that the changes are performing better and faster than the competition.

To get here, these organizations will need to develop the skills needed in analysis professionals to define and facilitate these processes. This is a far cry from where most organizations are at today, and where most analysis professionals are also at.

The barriers that lie in the way include

- an under utilization of the business analyst role organizationally,
- a lack of business analysis skills at many levels and in many roles of the organization, and
- a performance and budgeting structure that allows "developer utilization" to trump analysis and value delivery.

In an AI-first world, the critical path to solution delivery will no longer be the coding/development process, it will be the *analysis*. Deciding precisely what to do, and deciding between options, constraints, and other factors, will be paramount.

To make these decisions correctly, they will need tight analysis, research, modeling, and data-based evidence. And this must, and can, happen quickly! This analysis will need to be continuous, and not just a phase.

When AI is leveraged with analysis the results can be impressive!

Teams and individuals that have an analysis and value mindset are constantly looking for opportunities to use analysis in a nimble manner to meet strategic objectives. These teams and individuals see paths that others do not, and they can dramatically reduce costs and increase the value delivered.

Tim's Story

> While competing in triathlons, I witnessed how aligning to value is always the fastest route. Standing on the start line of the swim one time, I noticed that the race director had forgotten the starting buoy, which forces swimmers to navigate before the second and third buoys. While standing on the right-hand side as the gun sounded, a competitor started to run toward the sand peninsula that headed toward what would normally be the second buoy. In a flash, I realized this was not breaking any rules, and so I followed the running competitor. We hit the water well in front of the pack, navigating the mandatory buoys, and swam the shortest distance.

Strategic Thinking Using AI

Often when talking with leaders, we hear that ideas are plentiful. Once a senior executive said that there were so many good ideas being generated across their organization, but very few of them were implemented. Doesn't this mean they were not really good ideas? If they were, they would have been implemented. Every organization has a plethora of ideas, so what stops organizations from leveraging them?

The main reason is that there is often no distinction between these good ideas and other ideas. What is often missing from organizations is the evidence-based analysis, value analysis, and link to strategic intent. This is common within many organizations, where the analysis and measurements of success are not defined, and the leader who's best at socializing ideas often wins.

Business analysis is all about taking an idea, analyzing it against the current state of the organization, validating how good an idea it is, understanding the assumptions, and assigning value to it of introducing the change to the organization.

By assigning value to the ideas with a measurement of impact over time, a "good idea" can be truly assessed and ready for a decision. Once you have a valid predictive system to estimate each "good idea" and measure it, then each one can be ranked with more certainty that it will bring benefit to the organization. AI will also enable this process at lightning speed with the right analysis skills and **assets**.

For example, while reviewing a warehousing process and system, it was discovered that an ordering system for warehouse stock replenishment had been purchased and implemented. However, during its implementation, it was too difficult to interface the ordering system with the existing warehouse tracking system. Because of the lack of an interface, orders were re-keyed into the warehouse tracking system. The ordering system was costing the company thousands of dollars in licensing, support, hosting, and maintenance. While they were in the process of implementing the new warehouse system, the business process solution was to use a paper ordering book, costing $10, and turning off the non-interfaced ordering system. This is an example of a "good idea" implemented poorly to add negative value to the organization.

At the strategic level, AI will provide an opportunity for increased diverse thinking. Organizations are often constrained by either so many "good ideas" or not enough different ideas. If correctly prompted, AI will be able to provide a variety of new and different ideas, shaping new business models with alternative products and services. Diverse ideas will be generated in minutes rather than humanly workshopped over months.

Another limitation many organizations face is being able to validate "good ideas" quickly and objectively. AI will help business analysis practitioners perform validation on ideas, developing more precise ways of modeling what and how value could be realized for the organization by selecting an innovative idea.

In Chapter 2, we will introduce a framework that encourages strategic thinking using AI and enable the pieces to define, set up, and monitor AI-enabled processes. Processes that can be updated, enhanced, and changed quickly to enable rapid deployment and change to adapt to market conditions.

Chapter Summary

- Good business analysis is key for survival in the future as complexity and change accelerate with AI and other technologies.

- AI-first/enabled organizations need to integrate and elevate business analysis practices and skills throughout the organization.

- There is real importance in a rapid-learning knowledge workforce who are equipped with innovative business analysis skills.

Action Items

- Reflect on your (or your team/organization's) business analysts' current skillsets.
- Examine your existing business analysis practices in the context of the changing landscape of AI, complexity, and change.
- Observe how your organization uses strategic thinking with change initiatives.

These action items aim to guide individuals and organizations in adapting business analysis techniques to the dynamic business environment, fostering innovation and ensuring a competitive edge in the global market.

2 What Good, Bad, and Ugly Analysis Looks Like—Before and with AI

This chapter discusses how poor analysis is costing organizations and will cost more as we immerse in AI-enabled technology.

We also will discuss what good analysis looks like before an AI-immersed world, on the way into an AI-immersed world, and what we see fully immersed AI analysis looking like.

We look at why it is done so poorly in many organizations, and what needs to be fixed.

We introduce our **AI Analysis Accelerator Framework** as a guide to how good analysis should be performed to maximize value with technical advances like AI.

We will show how some organizations will leverage AI to stay ahead of competitors through insightful business analysis by leveling up their business analysis competency and capability.

Vignette

Samantha Ghent

In order to implement an analysis and AI-first-driven organization, I have had to really look at how we define the term "project." I realized early on that we had everything defined as a project, and often "projects" were getting split into multiple projects, isolating the technology or processes. This was causing us to have little to no view of the value streams and customer journeys and was completely cutting off our ability to align strategy and execution.

If analysis was only done within a tiny and isolated view of what we were calling projects, we found it was actually backfiring and causing more issues. For example, things like

- *analyzing and finding cost-efficiency solutions in one area, only to push cost to another area,*

- *optimizing the experience of one employee group, only to make the customer experience worse,*
- *not seeing how a huge backlog of defects and enhancements were continuing to fix the same customer journey from multiple points of view, constantly causing two business groups to re-do one another's "projects," and*
- *having our data quality suffer due to various groups using different definitions of simple terms, causing data to be used differently in a single customer journey, and different customer journeys, for the same customers (bad-quality data was causing poor decision-making as our reporting capabilities suffered, and, moving to an AI-first world, our AI would have suffered hugely if we did not fix this).*

Now we see a world where new product development (or a new internal process to support a new product or service we offer) are where "projects" apply. These projects and teams require strong analysis skills in the domains of product management and business analysis; overlapping skill sets. We now have career paths where these two skill areas are in the same career path area.

Business analysis is now less about a project and more about defining, aligning, and setting up a customer journey, then setting up the data, rules, processes, and tools to constantly monitor, update, and align the customer journey to strategic imperatives, and make sure small changes do not impact the customer journey negatively.

Current State: Most Organizations are Doing Poor or Average Analysis—and it is Costing Them!

Most organizations are wasting an immense amount of resources, money, and time by making changes with woefully inadequate analysis practices. Rushing through projects, software updates, compliance requirements, and process changes with a severe lack of analysis causes not only waste, but rework and residual problems. Many think the challenge is that they don't have time for analysis, and what they don't realize is that good analysis is done in parallel while working on change—it's not a phase before, it is continuous. Continuous analysis at various levels—strategic, initiative, and implementation—is needed to align the work to meaningful results.

As change and complexity accelerate, the concept that analysis can be done before the development, as a phase, becomes increasingly risky and inadequate. Dynamic and continuous analysis, assisted and augmented with AI, is the new norm.

> According to project-management guru Antonio Nieto-Rodriguez, some 88 million people will be working on projects worth $20 trillion by 2027. Yet, Nieto-Rodriguez concedes that "only 35% of the projects undertaken worldwide are successful—which means we're wasting an extravagant amount of time, money, and opportunity."[1]
>
> "Most change programs fail. In large organizations, the success rate of well-intended, carefully planned and well-funded change programs is somewhere around 20 percent."[2]

Poor analysis includes

- stakeholder analysis not being done well by business analysts, leaders, and/or project managers,

- the bigger picture being missed by not using techniques such as value stream analysis, customer journey analysis, and/or process analysis,

- missing and unidentified context, which creates missed impacts and residual problems that great business analysis catches,

- analysts being expected to "spec out" a solution handed to them, without proper analysis being done, and get "requirements documented" quickly so that development can start,

- heavy text-based documents being handed off from team to team, and

- far too much technical detail in the "requirements," causing development teams to implement what is documented rather than focusing on the need and problems to solve.

These poor analysis practices may have worked in the past, but, we would argue, they have never been the optimal way to do great analysis. Today's advancements and complexities no longer make these practices a viable approach.

1. Denning, S., "How Management Mediocrity Is Celebrated as Success." Forbes, 30 November 2021: https://www.forbes.com/sites/stevedenning/2021/11/30/how-management-mediocrity-is-celebrated-as-success/?sh=3093c6565c93

2. Denning, S., "Why Change Programs Fail: Ten Principles for Getting It Right." 29 March 2010: https://www.stevedenning.com/slides/GettingChangeRight-Mar29-2010.pdf

Continuing with any of these practices, no matter what your organizational hurdles are, will only keep delivery slow, compromise quality, and increase the friction between customers, business units, and implementation teams. Organizations not adapting are seeing and will continue to see painful consequences.

Here are some more details comparing good and poor analysis:

Good Analysis	Sub-Par Analysis—Costing Your Organization $$$
Backlogs are created through measuring customer, user, business, and systems processes, and seeing the problems and opportunities from these measurements. Business analysis is critical to finding these problems and opportunities before others report them. Items reported by users and leaders are researched with evidence-based data to quantify and qualify the issue for prioritization.	Backlogs are created through anyone submitting "requests" with everything from ideas, enhancements, defects, and more. No holistic backlog analysis maps the items to overall process performance to help prioritize.
Items are worked on based on value and impact, measurements, data, and evidence, and are analyzed and facilitated through business analysis.	Items are worked on based on the leaders' opinions and perceived urgency. The real issues and opportunities are often ignored, and the wrong solutions are implemented, causing rework later and missed opportunities.
Backlog is analyzed holistically, where most of the items "requested" are analyzed and removed due to them not being strategically aligned, or the same user action/scenario is already being worked on.	Backlog items are worked on one by one and connections between items are not seen. Items often create problems downstream for other areas or users. Lots of work is done with little bottom-line impact. In fact, much is done over and over again in subsequent requests.
Process **assets** are defined, mapped, and used along with data evidence and strategically aligned measurements to discuss, prioritize, and design improvements.	Requests are submitted with solutions already identified that are not questioned or analyzed. Options, alternatives, and the root causes are not examined. Much of this work is wasted or redone later in other requests when it does not meet user or business needs, or, worse, impacts other users or areas negatively.

Good Analysis	Sub-Par Analysis—Costing Your Organization $$$
Once an item is prioritized for implementation, the team works to confirm a shared understanding of the user, strategic alignment, and what some potential design options and alternatives might be. Lean experiments are run quickly to test assumptions and risk areas, and each user scenario is defined and modeled to create a shared understanding. Teams collaborate through the process together with a value perspective throughout, all the way through to end-to-end and UAT testing.	Once an item is prioritized for implementation, a solution is determined, and technical details are spec'd out to be handed to the development team.
Requirements are derived from value streams and customer journeys; understood as assumptions that might solve a business need or opportunity they are traced to.	Requirements and specs are mostly text based, lack structure, and are often full of technical team task-level details.
Test scenarios are user focused and are based on real business and user scenarios, prioritized by value, and automated to be run at any time. A change to the process or system creates a review of all the automated test cases to see what needs to change to cover the existing and new functionality.	Test scenarios and test plans are often created without a good understanding of the user process and user goals. Many test scenarios tested do not even apply to the business context. Critical test cases are often missing.

Poor and sub-par analysis practices will only hurt organizations in an AI-driven environment. They will create unneeded lag time, delays in implementing, errors, quality issues, rework, and mistrust among customers, business units, and implementation teams.

These poor practices are hindering the success of projects. Analysts are also at fault for not escalating this failure to senior management and not setting up projects well by executing well-structured business analysis plans. Many in project management and business analysis roles are simply not, or never have been, trained on effective analysis techniques and the mindset needed to succeed.

Often, analysts display a victim mentality: *It was not my fault—the project was a train wreck! I was restricted in the scope of the analysis I was able to perform...* While this might be true, it is not acceptable. Together, leaders and analysts can bring about better practices.

With GenAI now augmenting many analysts in their practices, poor business analysis can still happen. Some ways that misusing GenAI without the proper analysis skills can create poor analysis outcomes include

- not using GenAI to augment analysis at all,
- not understanding GenAI enough to help business leaders solve challenges with potential GenAI-enabled solutions,
- using GenAI to replace business analysis; it does not replace analysis, but it can augment and assist when used concurrently with analysis skills,
- not addressing the analysis and requirements process changes needed, as the SDLC changes, to leverage GenAI,
- not leveraging business analysis-specific skills, techniques, and analysis patterns as part of using GenAI; a highly skilled and trained business analyst will ask more sophisticated questions to enable GenAI results than an inexperienced and untrained business analyst, and
- using GenAI to write requirements without the analysis and collaboration skills to know how to use the outputs that it produces.

Why is Analysis Done So Poorly in Many Organizations?

There are a variety of factors that lead to analysis being done poorly in organizations, which we explore next, such as

- the wrong level of detail,
- a focus on the development critical path, and
- career path challenges.

The Wrong Level of Detail

Business analysis is done poorly in many organizations because it is performed at a detailed implementation task level rather than at a strategic high level within the enterprise, which is then connected to the detailed analysis. When this low-level analysis isn't connected to the high level, waste and mistrust easily happen.

Too many teams or analysis individuals are given an isolated solution to analyze or a technical component to analyze, rather than a problem to solve or an opportunity to develop results from. It's sort of like looking at everything with a hammer in your hand when you need a screwdriver. If the scope of what can be analyzed is constrained, so the results will be, at all levels of detail.

Misaligned accountability structures, and project management approaches have been mis-used over the last 30 years to split IT application areas, often relating to individual business units or systems, assigning business analysts to each area or system component. This has created silos and woefully inadequate business analysis, impacting the delivered value of projects to the business and customers.

Critical Path

Many organizations see development (programming and coding) as the critical path to getting to results, and what takes the longest duration of time on projects. Work plans are built around giving development enough time. Analysis is often seen as something that must be done in a hurried phase before development can begin and is often given little time. The analysis process is rushed and pressured to get done as soon as possible, so that development can start. Development is seen as "the real work" and as the "valuable" part of the process. This can put a lack of focus on ensuring the right thing is built and an artificial focus on getting to the build phase quickly.

In many ways, this is correct! Analysis, when done poorly, at the wrong level of detail, and without the correct skills and focus, is simply ineffective and wastes time. On the other end, rushing to code the wrong thing does not serve the organization either.

As technology becomes more complex and driven by dynamic AI, deep learning, and LLMs, analysis and requirements work needs to be done differently. It needs to be driven from reusable **assets** and continuously, not as a phase. Teams and organizations that can transform analysis practices into continuous improvement processes and asset-driven analysis models, will be able to enable speed, adapt more quickly, and leverage AI more fully with less rework.

With GenAI, and other AI advances, we believe that development will no longer be the longest task to complete on the critical path, and analysis will be. Analysis will need to transition dramatically in how it is seen, managed, and integrated into the work the organization does. Bad and ugly analysis will cost organizations even more.

GenAI can write code, enable more reuse of code than before, and enable more automated testing. If GenAI is used to generate the code and tests, and it has incorrect and incomplete scenarios (developed with a lack of analysis), then the outcome and completed solution will not align to create the intended **business results** and may actually make things worse. Yes, ugly and bad analysis can become even worse with AI! It can also get better, but that depends on how well your analysis skills and practices are used.

GenAI can be easily misused and applied to business analysis and requirements work in the same way. Without deep business analysis competency, using GenAI to augment business analysis work can be using the wrong tool for the context. Whereas, using GenAI with the right business analysis skills can amplify the analysis work and yield tremendous productivity and results.

Career Path Challenges

Traditionally, business analysis practitioners were developed into the role from many other professions, such as developers, testers, service desk support person, project support person, subject matter experts (SME), or a completely different role outside of information technology.

While all these pathways have been useful to build the profession, there have been some constraints because not every business analysis practitioner has had the opportunity to be trained in all knowledge areas, skills, and techniques of business analysis.

This lack of a career development pathway has meant that the quality of business analysis being performed is not producing the needed results. Being a subject matter expert (SME) has been a common pathway to becoming a business analysis practitioner. Intimate knowledge of a business unit has been a strength to the SME crossing over into business analysis. This has been observed with success from such roles as a nurse, logistics officer, bank teller, insurance officer, business operations, programmer, and many other detailed roles. However, too often, these SMEs do not develop the critical skills and competencies to see and analyze beyond their subject matter knowledge. They lack true analysis skills and techniques to help move the business forward, align to strategy, and have a holistic view to facilitate a diverse stakeholder group through change.

> For the last 30 years, business analysis practitioners have been almost exclusively active in the project delivery layer, leaving higher-level analysis incomplete. Focusing on delivery has meant there has been a shortfall of analysis being performed at a portfolio or strategic level. This has meant that there has been a huge gap in delivering strategy and delivering projects. Many organizations have experienced poor business analysis because the work being analyzed is not aligned to the strategic direction of the company.

Business analysis relies upon communication and influence skills just as much as analytical and critical-thinking skills. Most business analysts are comfortable with the technical side of business analysis skills, such as modeling, documenting, and associated tools. Some lack the critical-thinking and analysis skills to direct the right application of these technical skills. Many analysts struggle with the communication, negotiation, and leadership and influence skills that are so important to achieving the outcome required with senior management.

With GenAI augmenting business analysis work, and the need to consult with business units on how to leverage AI to solve business problems, many of the technical skills of documenting, modeling, and tools will be less important, and the critical-thinking and influence skills will become more critical.

What Do We Need to Fix to Enable AI?

Connecting Strategic Intent to Delivery

Good analysis connects even the tiniest detail to strategic intent, truly understanding and creating focus on solutions that deliver on strategic imperatives. Yet many business analysis practices, as discussed above, simply do not create this alignment. Most analysis is done in a silo and is not connected to strategic intent.

While no analysis is perfect, good analysis can get to a lot of these impacts while maximizing outcomes and minimizing wasted development.

Below we outline what this may look like:

	No AI	AI Assisted	Fully AI Enabled
Ugly Analysis Complete lack of strategic linkage in analysis work.	Detailed tech specs called "requirements" created by a BA as they take notes on what stakeholders say they need.	AI tools "write requirements" for the team or BA, but analysis doesn't really happen. Projects continue to fail and miss the mark.	Solutions are recommended by an AI agent, and decisions are made to accept or deny the change without proper analysis. Chaos ensues!

	No AI	**AI Assisted**	**Fully AI Enabled**
Poor Analysis Heroes may step up to create a linkage to strategic intent.	BAs do their best with a limited scope of analysis to create user stories or requirements documents. True analysis is lacking to align and measure the work to strategic imperatives.	BAs leverage AI to assist with creating requirements documents, user stories, and acceptance criteria, but are not having the high-impact conversations needed to get results; they are relying on AI too much without inserting true BA skills into the work.	BAs leverage data analytics and AI agents to recommend, develop, and test solutions, but problems after implementation plague the business and customer experiences.
Good Analysis Strategic linkage is part of the process, work, and skills.	Starts with the metrics and users, and decomposes user actions and scenarios; defining process, data, and rules. With this big picture, the right conversations happen to align results and code.	AI is used to assist the BA in providing context for the users and process, draft requirements, draft models, mock-ups, and assist the BA in getting at knowledge that previously took weeks of meetings with stakeholders to get at. The BA is able to work much faster and at a higher level of quality by using BA skills and techniques to utilize AI as an "assistant," but also knows the context and techniques well enough to guide AI for better results, and edit what AI provides.	The BA has set up a dashboard to measure the user and customer processes with real-time process performance metrics. The BA works with an AI agent to investigate, research, look at options, run prototypes, test, and present a proposed solution to stakeholders all in a very fast time frame. The BA utilizes **assets** created by AI, which are continuously updated and used to analyze and align to strategy.

Later in this chapter, and in subsequent chapters, we introduce the **AI Analysis Accelerator Framework** to make this connection happen within the context of AI.

Be Passionate About the Problem More Than the Proposed Solution

Many analysis efforts start with a proposed solution, and the analysis process never challenges the solution idea. This happens when a small group of leaders determine the solution and kick off a project, asking an analyst to get the requirements done for the already defined solution. When this happens, the focus on the problem is often lost in the rush to get requirements done. This often results in solutions that do not meet the actual business needs, and rework disguised as defects and enhancements are the norm for years.

As technology and change continue to accelerate, this challenge will become even more disastrous if left unchecked. We must get back to an approach that is focused on the problem or opportunity, not go straight to the solution implementation details.

AI that includes advanced data analytics and GenAI will enable a whole new way of monitoring and tracking customer, user, and business processes. With these newer AI capabilities, problems can be identified faster than humans recognize them, and potential solutions can be prescribed as well. Good analysis can set this up, track these issues and prescriptions, and use critical context (only humans would know) to facilitate decision-making and implementation of AI recommended solutions.

The funny part is that AI will replace the "leader" dictating a solution for a business analyst to work on, as the AI will detect the problem or opportunity much faster. Now, the question is, "How will your analysis skills stand up to AI?" The solution will not need to be detailed in a requirements document; the AI knows what to do. The analysis will need to determine whether the AI recommended solution is valid and worth implementing. The analysis will need to determine whether the AI has the context and user scenarios correct for the problem to be solved. The analysis will need to take the context into account and align the AI options to the strategic intent.

Focus More on Users and Customers

Leveraging AI to improve our customers' interactions with our organizations, and to make our internal users and business partners more effective, will mean more focus on the problem to solve and opportunity to target. This focus is not about technical problems to solve, but rather user and customer opportunities and problems to solve. Making internal users better at what they do and giving customers the hassle-free "easy button."

Solutions leveraging AI will require far less work to define the details in advance, and far more work to hypothesize and experiment, while keeping the strategic imperatives connected. This work requires structured analysis of the user behaviors, the users, and each user scenario impacted. This work requires business analysis skills and techniques to perform structured analysis and structured conversations to make decisions about these users and scenarios. While much of this has always been considered good analysis, most analysts have never been trained in these techniques, nor have they practiced them and developed true competency in them.

How Analysis Happens in Most Organizations, and AI's Impact

Below we describe a generic business analysis process and how it is changing.

	Before AI	With Some AI	Fully Enabled AI
Intake: Researching issues, defects, ideas, and enhancements, and determining which to work on.	Very few BAs do this work. Leaders, impatient for quick results, often meet without the BAs, and little analysis or evidence/data is used to make decisions. Leader knowledge and opinions drive decisions.	GenAI can be used to research common industry solutions and understand current business performance. Data analytics AI can be used to qualify and quantify the problem and predict how big the problem or opportunity will become.	BAs will collaborate with AI agents to leverage common industry knowledge, internal knowledge, and data to make better decisions and even identify opportunities and problems before human seven know about them. BAs and AI will work together to prioritize the items based on cost and opportunity. Analysis will be needed to ask questions of the AI agent to ensure a mutual understanding of the problem, opportunity, and solution.

What Good, Bad, and Ugly Analysis Looks Like—Before and with AI

	Before AI	**With Some AI**	**Fully Enabled AI**
Elicitation and analysis: Detailed interviews, conversations, and analysis in order to write user stories or a requirements document.	Conversations focus on detailed workflows and implementation details. The level of alignment to strategy and analysis quality depends on the level of skill in the person doing the elicitation and analysis work.	BAs use AI (GenAI and data) as an assistant to research business processes and stakeholders, accelerating conversations and elicitation. BAs use GenAI to draft visual models and mock-ups to analyze and ensure requirements gaps are identified. BAs use GenAI with deep analysis and prompting skills to generate needed documentation and edit as needed.	Many conversations are dramatically accelerated as GenAI and data analytics provide context, evidence, and recommendations. BAs use their analysis skills to work with AI agents and stakeholders to ask the right questions to make effective decisions on solutions to implement.
Review and approval: Reviewing the requirements and getting approval to move forward.	Text-based requirements are reviewed and discussed. More skilled analysts use visual models to facilitate the right conversations.	Reviews should go much faster as the technical detail should no longer be needed. The focus is on users, user actions, scenarios, process, data, rules, and alignment to metrics.	Documents, if needed, are created by GenAI, and BAs will validate for accuracy. BAs will need to prompt the AI agents in the creation of any documents to make sure that they are fit for purpose.

	Before AI	**With Some AI**	**Fully Enabled AI**
Support: Supporting the development, testing, and implementation.	Analysts are available to answer questions about details as the developers code, while testers prepare to test, and implementation details are completed.	With GenAI creating much of the code, and the test automation, BAs are needed to ensure that the right things are being tested and covered in the testing. User scenarios with expected results will be key.	GenAI and a more limited technical team develop, test, and implement. BAs are the facilitators of value in this process, holding the guardrails to align the work to the strategy. BAs are needed to ensure the quality of tests the AI is generating are appropriate for the right scenarios.
Measure results: Evaluating, monitoring, and measuring the solution effectiveness.	Rarely done today because in the rush to implement and the expense to set it up, the business process and user performance metrics are typically not set up to be monitored.	BAs start to *experiment* and dig into using data to monitor process performance.	BAs, with the help of AI, create dashboards to monitor metrics that align to strategy. Problems and opportunities are identified with speed as BAs and AI agents work together.

For many years, a large number of organizations have had business analysts and IT teams working on BAU (business as usual). Their backlogs of work are typically siloed by technology application or component. Backlogs come from defect reports, enhancement requests, change requests, and technical roadmaps.

Little analysis is done on the backlog as a whole, or on strategic alignment. Leaders are often prized for prioritizing what they think is most urgently needed. Business analysts, or other analysts, "spec" out the technical details.

Now, imagine a new (AI and analysis first) world where backlogs come from evidence and data insights that measure actual user performance using the products and performing the processes. What matters is actually measured and is measured ongoing. Improvements are identified and fixed far before anyone would even report the issue in the past.

What Good, Bad, and Ugly Analysis Looks Like—Before and with AI

Analysts interact with AI and facilitate a decision to accept or validate the data and recommended solutions from the AI input. Analysts use data analytics, observation, stakeholder conversations, and analysis techniques to facilitate these decisions. Items are prioritized based on the cost (positive or negative) to the organization that AI has calculated. Instead of writing specs, analysts have an AI-based conversation with a system to update it, and then run an automated regression and new tests to validate the changes. The decision to implement is based on the results.

The business analyst work performed here fundamentally changes. The role and mindset remain focused on facilitating business change as it always has. How this is done is changing fast.

BAU Yesterday	BAU Tomorrow with AI
System-based changes requested by users and business leaders.	Monitoring user and customer processes. Structured conversations with leaders about the process performance and business goals.
Backlog items submitted: problems, opinions, and ideas.	Evidence-based backlog items based on data and AI. Structured conversations with leaders about the process performance and business goals.
Prioritization based on leaders' opinions.	Prioritization based on data where AI calculates the real cost/benefit. Structured conversations with leaders about the process performance and business goals.

There are also projects that are about creating new products, systems, processes, and services. These are complex projects that are typically capital investment, enterprise impact programs.

Sometimes these get split out into a bunch of "technical projects." These projects have struggled for decades with analysis because the splitting into smaller projects makes end-to-end analysis extremely difficult.

BAU Yesterday	BAU Tomorrow with AI
Big program setup with multiple projects. Business analysis work is done on each project separately.	Programs are set up with end-to-end analysis and are aligned to strategic imperatives with well-aligned metrics. Analysis leverages GenAI and AI data analytics to drive evidence-based decision- making to ensure the right things are being worked on. Organizational **assets** are maintained with the help of AI and are used as input to analysis and interact with AI tools to design, implement, and test the right user scenarios, and measure the strategic alignment.
Projects organized by tech application, and business analysts assigned by application. Analysis done in a silo and managed from a technical point of view.	Smaller teams are organized by user metrics to optimize. Analysts and analysis are focused on managing a user experience point of view and metrics that bring the user experience together with business impact. AI is used to fill in the details with a careful eye from analysts, who can use analysis techniques to detect where AI may be off.

New development of products and services has traditionally had a few big metrics at the program level about the business objectives, and then, as the program has split into multiple projects, the focus became the individual application. This created a dynamic of losing the connection to the business outcome as projects were measured by outputs instead of outcomes and **business results.** With AI, we can now more easily measure and align the detailed work to the **business results,** but we need the right analysis framework in place to achieve this.

Now is the time that both BAU and new products and services are managed with analysis of outcomes and metrics that fully align to strategic intent.

Some teams claim their work is purely "technical" and they cannot align to users, customers, or organizational strategy. For example, we hear many teams say things like, "Well, I work on APIs, upgrades, or platform components that serve many teams, so measuring value and user experience really doesn't apply to us." This is exactly the type of mindset that must change.

These are great examples of things that can be measured from a value and user point of view, and should be, in most cases.

These technical pieces of work drive various success and failure scenarios that users and customers experience. Business and user value is impacted by these technical requirements, designs, and implementations. These technical aspects of our work contribute a significant amount to transactions and workflow traffic, creating positive or negative experiences for users and customers, costing or gaining the organization precious value.

An Analysis Framework for a New Era

With analysis as the new critical path, we need to rethink the approach for how we perform business analysis. The speed of change and use of AI will require a higher level of analysis skills, and will necessitate outcome-driven management, rather than output-driven management.

The focus from leadership and analysis professionals has to be on value in an AI-first organization. The balance between business results and customer obsession is critical. A business-results-only focus, with a lack of customer focus, will not yield the desired business results, and a customer-only focus, without alignment back to the business results, could easily have an organization go bankrupt. The two are analyzed in parallel and all the way from strategy to the details of execution. Good business analysis traces these with compulsion.

In the software-driven world, no longer can we build features that do not create value. Aligning deliverables to user behavior changes is key to creating business results. We believe that a key component to producing a business result is understanding customer journeys both internally and externally. Value streams and customer journeys are keys to understanding how features change human behavior that will bring about a business result. In AI-first organizations, value streams and customer journeys will become more and more important to derive business results.

The framework we are about to present has aspects of good analysis practices that have been proven for decades at various levels of context, and aspects of good analysis from many approaches and methodologies, outlined and popularized by others previously. Good analysis is performed at many levels by many roles within an organization, not just by business analysts.

To operate in the new AI-driven world, what we are advocating for is an analysis approach that brings together aspects of many traditional frameworks in a new way; to bring strategy to execution in a way that takes advantage of the complexity of organizations and systems, the speed of change happening, and enabling the pace that organizations will need to compete and deliver value.

You may recognize aspects of Lean, TQM, Six-Sigma, Agile, DevOps, and traditional software development frameworks. We also recognize that these concepts have also been popularized in parts by Joshua Seiden in *Outcomes Over Outputs*[1], Jeff Gothelf in *OKRs*[2], Results Chain[3], etc.

Business analysis happens in all of these frameworks. With AI, they can be effectively enabled and linked together with a holistic view to bring strategic analysis, operational analysis, value stream analysis, customer journey analysis, and systems analysis together into a single practice framework.

We are not looking to throw out any of these mentioned frameworks or methodologies; rather, it is about helping organizations integrate and connect them through powerful business analysis.

We are also not prescribing a new step-by-step framework or methodology; rather, a way of thinking that can be applied and leveraged in your organization no matter what frameworks or methods you are using. We are calling on business analysis to bring the various practices, views, and pieces together to help teams and organizations get results, rather than bringing another framework into play. We see business analysts as "integrators" of strategy, technology, and vision; along with the details of the people, processes, data, technology, rules, and systems. Together, these pieces—continuously analyzed as we work—make for a nimble and agile organization that can adapt and thrive in a complex and AI-driven world.

The critical elements of the **AI Analysis Accelerator Framework** are outlined below, and we will continue to define these in more detail, and draw out the connections and examples, in subsequent chapters.

| Assets | Hypothesis and Experiments | Team Tasks and Activities | Deliverables | User Behavior Changes | Business Results |

1. Seiden, J. Outcomes Over Outputs. 2019.

2. Gothelf, J. OKRs – Everything you need to know. https://jeffgothelf.com/okrs-everything-you-need-to-know/

3. For example, https://www.fujitsu.com/downloads/SVC/fc/fs/value-mgmt.pdf

Assets

 The foundation of analysis starts with **assets**. These are created, maintained, and used on an ongoing basis as business analysts facilitate various stakeholder groups through structured conversations. **Assets** are created in collaboration between a business analyst and AI, and then updated, discussed, and validated in collaboration with key stakeholders. Business analysts and the team use **assets** to discover gaps, create share understanding, and align their work to strategic intent.

Two key **assets** that will be discussed are value streams and customer journeys. These are both variations of process models that have unique views, often at a higher level, and focus on the customer and user experience, emotions, and behaviors. These models can be measured with data, leverage AI-based data analytics, and can be monitored in real time. They can have measurements tracked back to strategic intent. We can define these terms as the following:

- Value streams: The concept of "value stream" in this book may carry some slightly different definitions from those others use. We are describing value steam as a high-level model of how products and services are delivered to customers. A value stream is a high-level view of how additional lower-level processes and customer journeys join together to create value. Value streams have customers and are from an internal perspective.

- Customer journeys: These are external-facing processes that involve a customer. Customer journeys focus on the customer experience through their interactions in the delivery of products and services. Emotions and touchpoints are analyzed holistically and often include touchpoints outside of the product or system. These are key tools to understand **user behavior changes** as customers interact with the organization and products.

Assets include things like process models containing business rules, decision tables/trees, state transition diagrams, data flow diagrams, scope models, LLM source data and training information, user stories, use cases, acceptance criteria, user story maps, user scenarios, test scenarios and expected results, and prompting documentation. These **assets** typically describe the why, what, how, who, where, and when of the organization.

These **assets** you may recognize as traditional business analysis techniques. With AI, these are still needed, and more so! AI helps generate these **assets**, and a business analyst uses them to facilitate analysis, thinking, and the right conversations, when needed.

> The most important part is that with the more complex technologies and AI, these models and techniques need business analysts to have deep competencies to be able to co-create them with AI, and then facilitate the right conversations and analysis using them. Most analysts today are severely lacking in the skills to be able to do this.

The skills and competencies of utilizing **assets** and models for analysis must elevate in order to leverage them with AI. Business analysts must be able to

- understand each model/technique to know when to use it and in what situations,

- understand each model/technique enough to create effective prompts and conversations with an AI agent,

- understand the model/technique enough to edit the model draft created by the AI agent,

- understand that each technique can have different "views" and when to use various views, levels of detail, and work with an AI agent to create such a view, and

- understand that, with AI, an AI agent can create the model from a text (or voice) description, create it from reading code, or from the output the AI agent provides based on questions you ask.

GenAI can do amazing things to help us be more productive with these **assets** and models. But, in order to get these amazing results, there must be a foundational skill level that is higher than most analysts have to day with these analysis techniques.

Assets and analysis models are also no longer a "deliverable" as part of a requirements package; rather, an ongoing collaborative asset that the analyst owns, keeping them up to date and using them (even when AI generated) to facilitate the right decision-making and analysis with the stakeholders and team.

Hypotheses and Experiments

Hypotheses are statements that define provisional ideas of what might create a desired business result. **Hypotheses** are critical in an environment where complexity and change are the norm.

Every project has a desired business result, and this business result has an unstated **hypothesis** about how the project will create **deliverables** that "magically" create **business results**. **Hypotheses** remove the "magical mystery," and state clearly and transparently what the assumptions are about how an initiative, project, solution, or change is linked to getting **business results**.

An example **hypothesis**: We believe that if we create an AI-enabled chatbot to help with customers who're asking questions about their account, we will reduce call center volumes for account questions by 50%, which will reduce costs in customer service by 25%. We know we are successful when customers get their questions answered without exiting the chatbot process to "speak with a human" to get their questions answered.

Experiments are lean and short and are planned to quickly discover whether an assumption about users, customers, technology, or a process is what we believe to be true.

Changes to requirements, as requested by stakeholders, are often a **hypothesis** of what that stakeholder believes will create a desired business result.

Team Tasks and Activities

 Team tasks and activities are the **activities** that teams do to create the **deliverables**. The teams collaborate to design processes and systems, they implement code and/or configurations, they plan for tests and ensure the testing meets the expected results, and they collaborate with stakeholders to demonstrate progress and results.

These are the **team tasks and activities** that may typically show upon a project/task plan.

Deliverables

 Deliverables are the outputs the team creates. **Deliverables** are things like features, code, screens, implemented software, infrastructure created and configured, etc.

User Behavior Changes

 User behavior changes are the expected behavior changes that, when acted on by users, will drive **business results**. Some literature calls these "outcomes." It is common that a **hypothesis** is directly linked to a **user behavior change**. In the example **hypothesis** above, a **user behavior change** of customers successfully getting their questions answered without asking to speak to a "human" is the user behavior.

It is important that these are specifically related to human user/customer actions. Even the most technical work impacts the users in some way and some scenario, impacting what the user does or experiences. The users see something different, experience something different, and/or do something different than before. These user impacts are what drive actual **business results**.

Business Results

 Every project and work effort is undertaken to create **business results**. Most often, these are in terms of increasing revenue, decreasing costs, reducing risk, entering a market, or creating human prosperity. In order to link this business result to the work, we need to make some **hypotheses** about what user behaviors that when changed or improved will create this impact and business result.

Many project teams today are given business objectives related to cost reduction, risk reduction, or revenue increases. However, just because this is written in a project charter does not mean any further analysis or effort is taken to align this to the actual work being performed.

With AI advances, this connection between the impact and **business results** and the work being done by an AI agent and the team must be more transparent, visible, and connected.

Risks of Not Upping the Analysis Game

Organizations that do not level up their analysis game as AI implementation exponentially accelerates will face increasing pressure from customers, employees, and partners to elevate the user experience. These organizations will also face pressure from the increased competition, where the cost to produce will no longer be competitive as others are able to provide similar products, services, and quality levels for far less cost, and in far less time.

Traditional delivery methods, as well as the current agile norm of two-week sprints, will no longer be competitive. Many changes will need to happen much faster, and incremental changes that happen in hours, minutes, seconds, or milliseconds will be the norm, some organizations are already there. Continually prioritizing a backlog of features will also not be sufficient to provide the real changes necessary to be competitive in the marketplace. Decision-making on what to implement is starting to take a very different shape. Decision-making pace will be put into a spotlight in many organizations, and AI-augmented business analysis is the underpinning practice to prepare for these decisions.

The diagram below shows a traditional SDLC, and an agile one underneath. Implementation, for many organizations, takes at least two weeks in an agile process. However, AI is flipping both of these models into a whole new way of working.

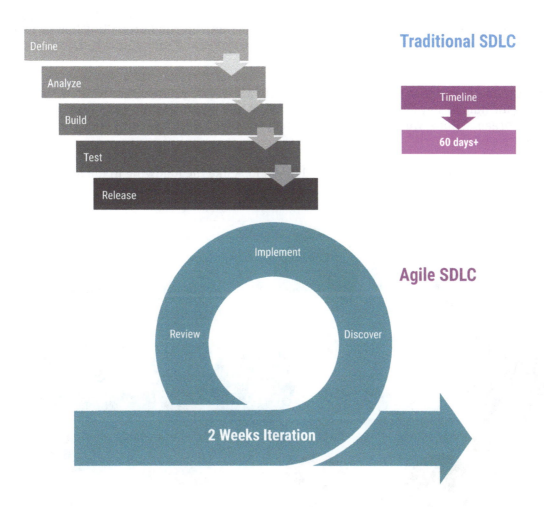

Leveraging AI Through Insightful Business Analysis

Leveraging AI with our analysis practices is not a choice, it's a matter of how well organizations implement it. If utilized correctly, AI could provide an opportunity for organizations to increase the value they deliver, minimize waste, and feel much more comfortable with how the work is aligned to deliver on organizational strategy, while allowing pivots as needed. AI and strong analysis provide access to new business models, new products, and ideas, and will enable delivery of them in record time compared to traditional and many agile models.

AI will help business analysis practitioners perform high-level analysis, and more quickly. This will develop more options and more thorough ways of modeling and predicting how to realize the value for the organization, allowing faster change cycles and more quickly delivering changes that resonate and deliver results.

Analysis and AI processes that are set up correctly will provide some organizations with a winning formula to stay ahead of the competition. While we are a while away from fully AI-enabled organizations, we believe business analysis will be a critical component for a competitive edge.

A potential delivery cycle that is AI enabled might look like the following in the future:

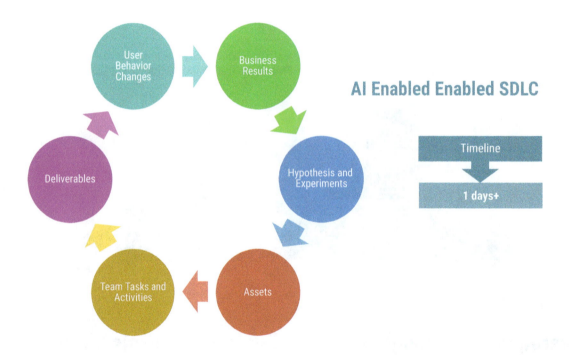

What Good, Bad, and Ugly Analysis Looks Like—Before and with AI

Chapter Summary

- The prevailing state of analysis in organizations is that many are performing at a poor or average level. This sub-par analysis will increasingly hurt the overall organizational performance as AI and complexity increase.

- This chapter explores the need to change business analysis activity from solely "delivery" to a strategic view encompassing an end-to-end perspective all the way to operations. It underscores the importance of aligning analysis practices with broader **business results**.

- Introducing an analysis approach tailored to the demands of the current and future era of AI, this chapter advocates for the reuse of patterns and discourages starting analysis from scratch.

Action Items

- Initiate an assessment of the current state of your (or your team/organization's) business analysis. Identify strengths and weaknesses in analysis practices and quantify the impact on **business results**. Use this assessment as a baseline for improvement.
- Look at what **assets** are currently used, and which need to be used and reused in your analysis practices.
- Recognize the risks associated with suboptimal analysis and develop strategies to up the analysis game. This includes understanding the potential consequences of poor analysis on innovation.

These action items aim to guide individuals and organizations in elevating their analysis practices, aligning them with strategic objectives, and leveraging AI effectively to stay competitive in the ever-evolving business landscape.

What Good, Bad, and Ugly Analysis Looks Like—Before and with AI

3 Understand the Past in Order to Navigate the Future

In this chapter we look at how business analysis practices have evolved over time. This history of why some of the current patterns and mindsets are in place in organizations can help us understand how to modernize them for AI.

We also go deeper into the **AI Analysis Accelerator Framework** and describe the concepts further as building blocks to AI-enabled analysis.

A new world of AI and analysis will require upskilling, and we begin to discuss this at the end of the chapter.

Vignette

Samantha Ghent

I am reading through the latest compliance requirement that we have 90 days to implement. We can get it done technically in one day, but the communications planning and strategy to leverage this compliance update as a competitive advantage is what takes time.

One of our business analysts is looking into this. She has our processes mapped, and AI is enabled. She can quickly analyze the compliance requirement and determine, with the help of AI, that it is a change to three existing business rules and adding one additional rule.

Using AI, our dev environment can calculate a risk factor in changing the three business rules, and they can run the 380 automated test cases that need to run to make sure the changes work and will not break anything.

She is also able to use plain language and the help of AI to add the additional rule to a mock production environment and run an entire month of production data against it. Then she will compare the results to last month to see if anything was impacted, and then run the new compliance reports and validate them, all in just a few hours' time.

How Did We Get Here?

Business analysis is an old activity. The first beginnings were performed in the act of bartering, starting around 6000 BC. Bartering required an understanding of value, quality, quantity, buyer needs, and associated risks or constraints to make sure that trading was successful. This meant that each individual would either have a good capability of business analysis or a poor capability, and those with poor capability in business analysis would miss out on obtaining the best and fairest trade that they could possibly receive. Education, skill, and experience would have been the keys to being successful in performing a higher level of business analysis while bartering.

Every organization around the world performs a degree of business analysis as every business, user, and system process gets defined, created, and changed. From high-level decision-making on the design of these business processes, to the fine details of how that business process works for a specific user scenario.

Purchasing a coffee, buying clothing, buying a car, choosing a school, buying a house... How much do I want to spend? Is it healthy? What is my personal taste? How many do I want? What quality do I need? What are the risks and constraints? Everyone has needs and requirements and makes prioritized decisions. Organizations that deliver products and services to customers, members, or citizens have needs and many requirements to allow these products and services to be successfully delivered.

As products, services, and the ecosystems that support business processes become increasingly complex and automated, analysis becomes more important. Analysis, deep analysis skills, and thoughtful organization of **assets** become paramount for survival.

In the last chapter we introduced the **AI Analysis Accelerator Framework** to help us understand the key concepts we need to understand to enable good business analysis in an AI-immersed organization. We introduced the concepts of **assets**, **business results**, **hypotheses and experiments**, **user behavior changes**, **deliverables**, and **team tasks and activities**.

Let's look further at a retail industry example to understand how we get from intended strategy and **business results** to the **deliverables**, **team tasks and activities.** In the example below we outline the chain of concepts that help us get from the desired **business results** to the needed work to be done. It is business analysis that facilitates completing the chain and alignment from the work being done to the **business results**.

Retail example

Business results: Increased sales (revenue) for the retailer.

User behaviors Change: People purchase products.

Deliverables: The systems used to purchase and transact.

Team tasks and activities: The things teams do to develop and keep these processes and systems running to enable transactions.

Assets: Knowledge of the team, existing processes and systems, rules, data and policies. Analysis **assets** like value streams, customer journeys, process, and visual models.

This is a more complex context than the historical system of bartering; it requires more people, activities, and tools to create outcomes and impact. We can start to see how the increased complexity of the many people, processes, and systems involved can start to create risk. We can also start to see how it is seemingly easy to assume and not discuss the **user behavior changes** and go straight from **business results** to **team tasks and activities**.

For such a young profession, business analysis has made huge progress in the connection between business needs and software. In the future the profession needs to continue the steep trajectory of skill development to service the required demands.

The Development of the Analysis Profession

With the formation of the International Institute of Business Analysis (IIBA) in 2003, business analysis developed as a profession. Now there is a professional guide to techniques, tasks, and associated competencies, which make the act of business analysis much more repeatable and of a higher quality. Just like some analysis skills were needed to barter 8,000 years ago, today these skills are much more formalized, complex, and need a lot of practice to master. Good business analysis practices can literally save organizations precious time, dollars, and risk. Business analysis is more relevant today and will be in the future in order to get quality of business outcomes. Fifty years from now, the core skills of business analysis will still be relevant in the age of AI and automation.

What is amazing is that although business analysis as an activity has been part of our everyday lives, it has not had a formal mechanism to make it easily taught to others. This has only been successful since the development of the *A Guide the Business Analysis Body of Knowledge (BABOK® Guide)* V1.4 in 2005, V1.6 in 2006, V2 in 2009, and V3 in April 2015.

> *BABOK® Guide* is the *Business Analysis Body of Knowledge*, written by a large group of practitioners based on a role delineation study of 1,000s of business analysis practitioners. It was published as the "Standard" for the profession by International Institute of Business Analysis™ (IIBA®) .

Before the formalization of the profession by IIBA in 2003, previous business analysis knowledge came from the likes of consulting firms, small boutique training companies, and specialized methodologies like Six-Sigma, Lean, and various software development methodologies.

The idea of business process improvement and software development teaches similar analysis methods and techniques, where business process improvement is seen as a "pre-step" and higher-level activity compared to systems implementation. Merging the analysis of business processes and systems seems so natural yet is not common practice. This must change because in a complex, technology and AI driven world, these are inseparable! Some analysts have been merging these disciplines for decades with huge success, but many have not yet taken this approach.

Laying the foundation for AI and modern business analysis is about data and users. The history of technology and the analysis role in it is largely dependent on understanding the information that users provide, how systems interpret, transform, and share that data, and how users consume data. Business analysis has always been about this, and this does not change with AI. What has changed over time is how much of this is automated, and the volume of data stored and shared. AI exponentially increases the amount of data that is used in automations and shared with users.

Business Analysis of the Past

Business analysis as a profession developed from the problems/issues encountered in developing software and making software useful to users. In the late 1900s, software became part of business, organizations became more dependent on it, yet developers often missed critical requirements. The challenge of building software efficiently and that actually made users better off has always been around and continues today.

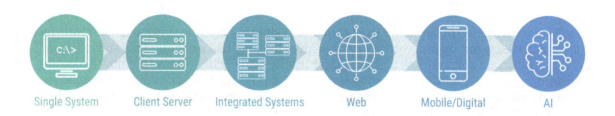

| Single System | Client Server | Integrated Systems | Web | Mobile/Digital | AI |

The role of "systems analyst" and/or "analyst programmer" was born out of frustrated users and programmers being tired of software being built that nobody used because it was not what they actually needed to improve their work process. Systems analyst and/or analyst programmer roles typically supported a single system and user group, they often used domain knowledge to get the work done, and although some analysis was needed, many could get by without the robust analysis skills we know of today. Their systems were mainly standalone and did not share data with other systems. Domain knowledge of the business operations and system was enough to get by. Yet, challenges persisted as there continued to be a huge gap in understanding between the needs of the business and the software and technology that was built.

What does this part of history mean to the goal of business analysis?

- *Users did not feel that developers understood their workflows.*

- *Programmers implemented systems and were frustrated when users often didn't love it.*

In the 1980s, relational databases and client/server technology with object-oriented development became the norm. Systems became more complex as data started to take on a new purpose and sharing data between systems started to become a strategy on the horizon.

Large, complex systems required a structure to enable the coordination of analysis, design, development, and testing. These models became a common language for use between teams. Systems analysts and business analysts started to use structured analysis techniques to help better design and architect complex systems with more complex data usage and processing.

What does this part of history mean to the goal of business analysis?

- *Users did not feel that developers understood their workflows and how they used the data and needed to use data downstream.*

- *Programmers implemented systems and were frustrated that they weren't told some of their requirements; the business/IT friction starts.*

In the 1990s we started to see some integration of systems and the invention of user interfaces, which made it easy for anyone without system knowledge to use systems. This started a whole new era of business and systems analysis. User interactions with systems are now becoming important as more use software. Client-server systems and relational databases enabled more complexity and shared data among more user groups, and more and more non-technical users were using software. It was now becoming less common to see large physical filing cabinets of documents, paper containers, and file bins on everyone's desks in offices.

In an effort to be more "efficient" with expensive "software engineering," many organizations—for large and complex project work—isolated the analysis into a phase before the development. The business analyst role started to become independent from a programmer. Making the programmer role efficient was a strategy, and systems development could be phased where requirements analysis and design happened ahead of time with less propensity for change. With stable requirements, a programmer could take a design and program efficiently. This stability of requirements didn't last long! As long as an exponential rate of technology change is happening, requirements will also change.

What does this part of history mean to the goal of business analysis?

- *Users struggled to define their requirements, and business analysts filled the gap, but not all analysts were well trained, and users still struggled.*

- *Programmers implemented systems, and the shared data impacted other users in negative ways, creating problems and missed requirements. Rework ensued.*

Out of the big consulting firms in the 1990s came several different software methodologies. Each one of these had roles that included systems analysts or a generic analyst. At this time, some of the first iterative methodologies started to gain popularity.

Next, the World Wide Web came upon us, and even more systems integration happened, where systems "talked" and passed data to one another. Even more everyday users were using technology who had not done so before. We saw more and more "internal business automation" happening, and more development for external users and customers. While software products really started to grow, the field of product management paralleled business analysis. Product management focused on software products that organizations sold or that were a required part of using another physical product. Business analysts were focused on helping internal systems, and systems that customers could optionally use.

What does this part of history mean to the goal of business analysis?

- *External users become more of a focus, external users performing self-service to get their needs met while reducing organizational cost. Competitive advantage enters the picture rather than pure "internal user efficiency" user goals. The customer experience with externally facing applications becomes an efficiency gain and a competitive advantage.*

- *Programmers' time becomes a driver of project pace. Many programmers are inexperienced and demand detailed spec-level requirements to meet their pace goals. Teams often lose the user focus and tie back to business goals.*

In 2001, the agile manifesto (www.agilemanifesto.org) was created to address the challenges of software development. Agile is about accelerating the feedback loop with smaller development cycles. Core to the manifesto was to create working software faster through collaboration and feedback cycles. Many popularized agile practices were around long before the agile manifesto, and many developed since. When implemented well, they can uphold the agile values and ways of working to enable agility.

What does this part of history mean to the goal of business analysis?

- *Teams were often skipping analysis to focus on "the agile process"; in reality, they misunderstood what "the agile process" was about. Analysis is part of agile!*

With the emergence of the IIBA in 2003, the roles of business systems analyst and business analyst became more prevalent, popping up in many organizations. The roles became the connection between the business needs and functioning software. This was born from the continuing need to ensure that business changes, process changes, and software functionality were relevant and delivered value. Increased complexity of software implementations was also driving this need for more analysis as more and more processes were automated, connected to one another, and sharing data. Without good analysis, new systems and system updates can easily cause more problems than benefits to various user groups.

At this time, it was rare for a system to "stand alone" and only be used by a single user group. Now, the data movement was in full swing. Organizations started to embrace automation and complex systems to share and store massive amounts of data. When data is shared between systems and processes, this complexity requires an immense amount of analysis (user, actions, process, data, dataflow, rules) to create the value that organizations are looking for and with the needed data quality levels.

With digital transformations, we have seen that the line between internal and external users is blurred, and, in many cases, these should no longer be separate systems like they were previously! Product management (typically for external customer-purchased software) and business analysis (typically for internal business users and customer-facing applications for servicing customers), both work on delivering value to users, often through technology, making them more efficient and helping provide better business and user outcomes. These two disciplines are blurring; they are essentially practicing a similar set of skills and tasks with a similar outcome. They both aim to build software that makes users better off than what they had before.

What does this part of history mean to the goal of business analysis?

- *Digital transformations are just as much about the users changing their actions and behaviors as they are about the technology changing. Many organizations have missed the user change part of this, which comes out in good business analysis. If the analysis is purely focused on the technology specs, the user needs are neglected, and the users choose not to use the new technology.*

Some organizations have developers do the business analysis, and many organizations, especially larger ones, have segregated the roles. This segregation has led to segregating the software development process.

This separation of "phases" of the software development process is one of the largest missteps in the history of business analysis practices. It has created silos and a lack of end-to-end analysis enabling alignment to strategic intent. It has isolated the role to a narrow scope of analysis that is often causing efficiency in one area but pushing problems to another.

As agile methods flooded the marketplace, some evangelical agile-ists rejected the role of a business analyst, with many thinking they could assume this role. While everyone does business analysis, this does not mean everyone does it well. Many agile coaches and trainers missed the fact that agile teams still perform aspects of requirements engineering, which has been performed well by many skilled practitioners in the business analysis community. Many development teams do not have these skills.

User stories and use cases are about users doing an action with an object for a compelling reason. Every requirement's best practice, since the 1980s, has been about users + action + object, and the value it has! Back to the bartering days some 8,000 years ago? "I need to wash my clothes and you have the tools I need, so can I use your tools to wash my clothes in exchange for cooking your family dinner?"

The agile business analyst role emerged; however, it was confusing to many. Many made it about a method rather than describing the role, mindset, and skills needed. It is a bit like calling a bartender a beer bartender when they can also serve wine and spirits. I guess this would be good marketing if you owned a brewery.

User stories should be about user outcomes and what makes a user successful, and mostly they are about the structured conversations that take place between team members (technical and not). But, many teams are failing at this and making them about documentation and outputs of what needs to be built. User stories should be mapped to product visions and metrics that show clear metrics to **business results** and **user behavior changes**, with clear strategic alignment. Many teams have no line of sight of this type at all.

"Data business analyst" has become a recent role (and title) in some organizations; however, like the agile business analyst, this role is confusing. All business analysts should work with data. And any data expert needs to understand who is using the data, and what are they using it for. Data, process, and business rules are three important components of the business architecture of an organization. Data analysis has become increasingly more important as more and more data is being used within the world of business. More importantly, those performing business analysis can effectively work with the data engineers, understand the source of the data, the data flow, and the quality impacts of the data for users and needs downstream. This is business analysis.

The Emergence of a New Complexity in Analysis

With AI taking a front seat in how organizations interact with customers, internal employees, and partners, and with improving productivity, a new complexity in how analysis is done enters the scene.

AI amplifies the risk and reward for doing good business analysis. It can amplify the collaboration of decision-making with analysis.

Imagine a time when the internet or a mobile phone was such a foreign and new concept. We remember back in 1999 reading one of those "chain emails" going around describing what we will be doing with our phones within 20 years. Things like banking transactions, watching/sharing/creating videos, and many things we take for granted today but which were laughable ideas back then.

The world of AI is full of examples where we hear about things that seem incomprehensible, they seem like sci-fi, and not things that will happen soon! Or will they?

In the rush to leverage AI, we must also practice good analysis to ensure we are not wasting money. But, rapid learning and experimentation is also needed to get ahead. Good analysis balances learning and **experiments** with analyzing for value and strategic alignment.

Back in 2008, the idea of a "mobile app" was brand new, and organizations spent millions to rush to create an "app" for customers to use on their mobile devices. A huge percentage of these apps back in 2008–2010 were huge failures! Why? Because it was a rush to create an app, an output, rather than creating value. Many organizations have spent millions of dollars redoing their apps since 2009, trying to get value to the users.

The rush to use technology without value analysis and alignment can cost organizations a lot of time and money. This learning cycle must speed up and allow learning to be valuable rather than wasteful. Good analysis enables this. Unfortunately, many organizations have still not learned these key mindsets, skills, and approaches to change, work, and software.

AI without analysis is analogous to this. We must have a structured analysis practice to ensure that we are spending our time and resources in a manner that actually delivers on strategic imperatives.

AI will move organizations quickly in a direction. For some organizations this will be advantageous, for others it will be a disaster.

AI Analysis Accelerator Framework—Accelerating Continuous Value in an AI World

Good business analysis in the age of AI focuses on value. Value is the result to the business; increased revenue or decreased expenditure.

So, how does this work with the following six key components of the **AI Analysis Accelerator Framework**? Let's dig in!

Assets   Hypothesis and Experiments   Team Tasks and Activities   Deliverables   User Behavior Changes   Business Results

To enable results to be realized, business analysis must consider the **assets**. All organizations deliver products and services through value streams, customer journeys, rules, data, and people in a location or locations. Getting these key delivery objects right is the pathway to organizational agility. As AI will orchestrate the value streams, customer journeys, rules, and data quickly at scale, it is critical that these are right. Business analysis done well achieves this result.

In an AI-first organization, **hypotheses and experiments** using existing **assets** can run quickly to predict likely results. Business analysis tasks, techniques, and competencies will need to change to enable highly efficient problem-solving for experimental modeling.

In the new AI world, **team tasks and activities** for developers will shift from writing large volumes of code to piece code and infrastructure together, alongside business analysis practitioners guiding the delivery. Creating fast demos and prototypes with codeless apps, business teams and analysts will model future option scenarios with descriptive and predictive data, evaluating test scenarios and making updates. Agility will be based on the cycle of building theoretical prototypes, measuring the outcomes, evaluating and readjusting.

Old **deliverables** of mass documentation will be obsolete as value streams, customer journeys, rules and data will be enough for AI to deliver working software. Value-added outputs are likely to include prototypes, **experiments**, code sets in test environments and live, automated test results and predictive value stream performance data.

Human **user behavior changes** are key, so business analysis practitioners must know how to measure these accurately; behaviors such as purchasing, repurchasing, and referring. Our job as business analysis practitioners is to align product features to increase changes in customer behavior. Working on those features that affect positive customer behavior will yield the best result for the organization.

The **business results** in most cases will be easy to see if measured in financial results of revenue and expense.

This connection is shown in the following diagram.

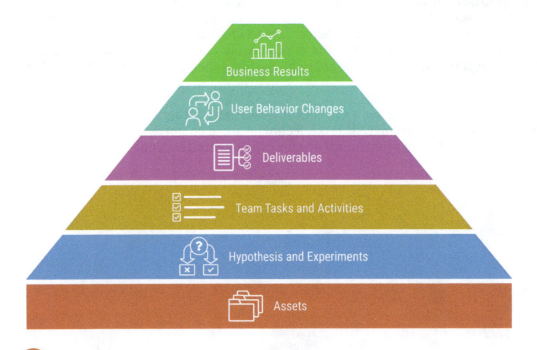

Understand the Past in Order to Navigate the Future

All of this creates a value stream and customer journey! This is what business analysis defines, enables, monitors, and helps organizations make changes to, to keep value intact and improve value creation for customers, employees, and the organization as a whole.

Organizations that are managing the value streams and customer journeys as a critical path will not only deploy changes faster, but they will deploy changes that are more valuable and competitive than other organizations.

In an AI-first organization, **hypotheses and experiments** using existing **assets** can run quickly to predict likely results. Business analysis tasks, techniques, and competencies will need to change to enable highly efficient problem-solving for experimental modeling.

The Skills Gap and the Urgency to Upskill

Nobody has these skills yet, but it is, by definition, business analysis. And things are moving so fast with AI that everyone has a skills gap!

The skills to thrive are advanced, and most business analysts have barely been trained on the basics. Some have been trained, but many are not using the skills for various reasons. Some are not simple to learn. Let's call them a set of competencies. They are skills that are complex and are not procedural. Even the best training courses are just at the beginning, to gain real skills and competency, one must practice and apply the skills in multiple situations, contexts, and fail—catching our own mistakes before truly mastering a skill.

Few organizations have empowered and enabled this type of skill development in their talent pool. So, why do some analysts (maybe 10%) thrive? Because they have a growth mindset, are okay pushing the boundaries, and are willing to fail to learn. But, this isn't the norm.

Continuous learning, incremental upskilling, and practice need to be the norm to upskill knowledge workers and build skills.

Business analysis is an advanced skillset that is built over years of practicing applying the skills to various situations, learning and trying again, then with different inputs and context, and again.

The organization that obsesses about learning will thrive in the age of AI. Learning patterns will shift from large-format learning to bite-size chunks every day. Like incremental software installs, learning will be a daily habit.

As technology moves at a faster pace, learning, unlearning, and relearning become extremely relevant. In the future, learning something new is going to be a daily activity. In fact, we predict that it will be a necessity to perform most jobs. Upskilling is about continuous learning, which is needed to go through the skill development process.

Thriving Organizations

Continuous analysis (not a phase) is also a critical shift in the future state. Organizations and business analysts that foster continuous analysis of value streams and customer journeys will no longer feel the need to have an analysis phase that takes up precious time to market and time to deploy. These teams will model potential solutions in mere minutes, taking full advantage of AI. More on this in the next chapter.

The time to validate all the automated testing scenarios and results are, in fact, what the business team would like to meet their goals and what will become a critical path. As automation takes over, testing speed increases, becoming simple and efficient.

Data analysis is emerging as the key focal point for business analysis, as rich datasets provide the key insights into descriptive and predictive data for customer behavior.

Chapter Summary

- This chapter emphasizes the need for a comprehensive understanding of business analysis evolution to navigate the challenges and opportunities in the future.

- The relationship between AI and business analysis has illuminated how current patterns and mindsets must change to take advantage of the changing landscape.

- This chapter further describes the **AI Analysis Accelerator Framework**, demonstrating how it can be leveraged.

Action Items

- Review how you or your team/organization is prepared for the business analysis evolution required to navigate the challenges and opportunities in the future.
- Evaluate your existing skillset, or team/organization's skillsets, and identify gaps related to the integration of business analysis and AI.
- Assess whether you are using components of our **AI Analysis Accelerator Framework**.

These action items aim to guide individuals and organizations in addressing the skills gap, leveraging the potential of AI within business analysis methods, and establishing a workforce capable of navigating the complexities of the evolving analytical landscape used for innovation and market leadership.

4   Future State—Analysis is NOT a Phase!

In this chapter we look deeper at a concept mentioned earlier, that of analysis not being a phase, but rather a continuous activity of change in an organization.

We look at the drivers for needing continuous analysis, and how this contributes to speed of delivery. We also look at how our **AI Analysis Accelerator Framework** enables continuous analysis and look at some examples of different types of projects where the framework concepts, AI, and continuous analysis manifest.

This chapter also introduces the paradigm shift needed to make the change into a continuous improvement and analysis practice and mindset.

Vignette

Samantha Ghent

With code no longer the critical path to deploy new software, changes, or much of the work we do, I really had to look at what the critical path now is and look to optimize it.

Coding now rarely happens with hands on a keyboard—most of our code is AI generated and assisted. What we learned is that this works well when we understand what we are trying to develop and achieve at an entirely different level than before. We found analysis is the critical path, yet making it a phase does not work. It's about continuous analysis and the assets we have as inputs for the hypotheses and experiments.

Continuous Improvement and Analysis is Intuitive

 The better we get at something, the more we take the freedom to change exactly how we perform it. For example, imagine the first time you cooked a complex recipe that you have now cooked several times and have memorized. The first time you followed the exact recipe, and you may have even phased it out by first getting all of the ingredients and supplies out, then chopping and measuring, and then finally digging into the step-by-step actual cooking of the recipe. After you have done it for a while, you know that during the cooking process there is some downtime, what can be done during those times, at the last possible moment. Every time you cook this recipe, you get more efficient and better at judging the timing and steps to make it great.

Analysis can be quite similar. If we are too phased with it, we end up having slower progress, and less ability to adapt to changing circumstances; we are not learning as we go. The solution quality is at risk, since we are somewhat blind to context and clues as we work. Following a phased, sequential process over truly engaging with our purpose and outcomes along the way can easily happen.

Good business analysis on projects and products has never been about it being a phase, yet many organizations, teams, and professionals treat it like a phase and get sub-par results. The hardest part is that these sub-par results are typically not understood until months down the road and may not even be tied back to an analysis challenge.

Good analysis has always been about being continuous, iterative, and layered to maximize value, quality, and efficiency, yet few organizations, teams, and individuals are performing at this high level.

So, how did so many teams and organizations stray from this? How did analysis become a phase for so many? Big, bulky, waterfall methodologies—are they the culprit? Maybe. We would argue that they are not, but we also see the pattern and attribute it to these methodologies being applied incorrectly, much like so many people apply agile ways of working so far from the intentions for over 20 years after the agile manifesto.

The future will only bring us more changes, more complexities, and more context that makes this a larger piece of the puzzle. Organizations, teams, and individuals treating analysis like a phase will only be met with dismal results.

Analysis happens at multiple levels of context and abstraction, and this is key to ensuring that the details align to the bigger picture and strategic alignment. The traceability from a strategic measurement of success to the details of what we want coded or implemented in a process should be obvious and transparent.

> With AI capabilities impacting not only external customer journeys, value streams, and our own work processes at a rate of change and complexity unseen in the past, we must work with a continuous improvement mindset and approach.

Continuous Improvement—Continuous Analysis

 Continuous analysis is the practice of defining, analyzing, measuring, and then modifying a process against defined success measurements. Compared to a project or product backlog-based approach, with continuous analysis we are constantly measuring what matters and the measurements inform us of where to focus improvements.

With AI today, we have greater capabilities than before to set up these measurements, maintain them, and use evidence-based data to make good decisions. AI, specifically in data analytics, along with good analysis is the key to making this a reality.

Each value stream and customer journey must have continuous measurements set in place that are constantly being measured and monitored. Much like business operations and systems operations have for years, AI capabilities allow us to more easily monitor and measure customer journeys, both external and internal end-to end performance, and allow us to harmonize human and AI intelligence with data insights and root cause analysis of where to improve the process.

Continuous analysis, partially automated with AI, amplifies measurements, analysis, and monitoring at the value stream and customer journey level. We still need humans with analysis skills and techniques to

- define these value streams and customer journeys and deeply understand the users, inputs, outputs, steps, and rules of them,

- define and align the measurements that matter in a value stream and customer journey and ensure these are strategically aligned to the organization's strategy at various levels,

- understand the data flow, inputs, and outputs to deeply understand where data quality is at risk, and address data-quality issues across the value stream and customer journey,

- set up and monitor dashboards for each value stream and customer journey, and analyze when action needs to be taken to **experiment**, modify, amplify, and test process variations, and

- define **hypotheses and experiments** and run them with an eye on the customer experience, user experience, data quality, and overall alignment.

What we are looking at here is a fundamentally different way of using business analysis skills in organizations.

It is switching from a project-based approach to continuous analysis. It is about optimizing our improvement efforts and resources while better seeing the big picture and strategic alignment.

An Example of Continuous Analysis

Imagine an example of a medical clinic with online booking of appointments. This is a capability that has been around for many years for some organizations, yet is new for others. It is something that the solution to book an appointment online would have a tech stack with: frontend, external-facing user interactions, APIs, data, backend processes, and more.

First, let's look at what may commonly be happening in many organizations. For many, the request and implementation process may resemble the following steps:

1. A business leader might see lackluster performance of this process after many complaints and issues.
2. They would need to submit a request to IT, often with a predefined solution in the request.
3. The request might be investigated, and eventually get into a prioritization meeting.
4. Some broken process would try to scope and estimate the project without any real analysis of the problem to solve.
5. Once prioritized, it would get assigned to a project manager or scrum team.
6. A business analyst might be assigned to "write requirements."
7. The team and stakeholders pressure the analyst to get requirements done fast so that coding can start.

8. The project is managed based on scope, schedule, and budget, defined without much analysis.

9. When the project is implemented on schedule, budget, and scope, the team celebrates.

10. The business and external users become frustrated as the new solution pushes issues to other users and does not fulfill the true intentions or value needed.

11. The business and users submit request after request to fix little aspects of the solution that get implemented one by one, creating an even bigger mess.

Now, let's look at how the **AI Analysis Accelerator Framework** can be used to enable AI and a continuous analysis approach.

Assets   Hypothesis and Experiments   Team Tasks and Activities   Deliverables   User Behavior Changes   Business Results

An AI and business analysis-first mentality, incorporating our six key components, would mean the following:

1. The business analyst investigates the value stream and the customer journey of appointment booking. They see that the data on the process performance is signaling issues the day after a new scheduling tool was put in place. AI-enabled data analytics shows real-time data variances on the process and the success measurements of the process. The analyst sees that a large number of patients are abandoning the scheduling process compared to last week. No issues have actually been reported. The analyst also notices that the call center has experienced a high increase in calls to make appointments. This is continuous monitoring and proactive analysis! The analyst is using **user behavior changes** to measure process performance.

2. The analyst also has these measurements that they are monitoring mapped to higher-level impact measurements, like revenue, cost, and risk. Models are showing the analyst that these measurements are leading indicators that revenue is at risk if appointments are not successfully made, patient health is at risk if patients are not seen, and costs are at risk to increase if call center volume goes up. The analyst has the **user behavior changes** mapped to the organizational **business results**.

3. Upon a small amount of research of the newly implemented scheduling tool for clinicians, the analyst asks a GenAI tool for a summary of what was implemented. The AI says that a key business rule implemented is that the scheduling tool only allows a scheduling window of three weeks out for clinicians to request time off. Most appointments are fully booked four weeks in advance, with 10% held for emergency appointments.
4. The analyst makes a **hypothesis** that this is what is creating the issue.
5. They ask the GenAI tool to model how many appointments would have been successfully scheduled if the rule was six weeks based on last month's data.
6. The analyst runs this **experiment** and finds that a significant percentage of appointments fit this window. This is all done in a matter of minutes, and the analyst can recommend the fix to the problem that many business leaders did not yet know was an issue.
7. The fix is approved and implemented, and automated testing is run. The fix is deployed.
8. The analyst also asks GenAI to write a notification to all patients who had tried to schedule and abandoned the process to please try again.
9. The notification is sent to the customer service manager for edits and then sent to impacted customers.
10. The analyst continues to monitor the process performance.

What a difference!

Older Way of Working (Not AI-Enabled) Deliverables	Newer Way of Working (AI-Enabled) Continuous Analysis
Objectives, OKRs, and business goals— handed to the analyst. Solution idea given to the team.	Metrics of **user behavior changes** to improve, monitor, and predict are aligned to strategic **business result** imperatives. Analyst performs AI-assisted research, data insights, and recommendations of what needs to be improved, and the impact of current issues.
Scope document/statement (hopefully a scope diagram)—jointly created by the project manager and business analyst.	Customer journey to improve along with the **user behaviors** of that journey to improve— already created as an **asset**, or created by business analyst facilitating team to create. AI may assist in creating an initial draft. Business analyst facilitates **hypothesis** with stakeholders.

Older Way of Working (Not AI-Enabled) Deliverables	Newer Way of Working (AI-Enabled) Continuous Analysis
• Requirements document • User story map • User stories and acceptance criteria • Visual models • All to be "approved" to move forward for a sprint, increment, release. Created by the business analyst in collaboration with stakeholders, facilitated sessions by analyst. Review and approve sessions with stakeholders, team, and analyst.	AI-assisted creation and analysis of organizational **assets**: • Value stream maps • Customer journey maps • Process/workflow models • Decision tables • User scenarios • User stories and acceptance criteria • State transition diagrams • Sequence diagrams • Wire frame flows • Screen designs Analyst chooses what is needed and uses AI to draft them based on prompting or existing code. Analyst analyzes the AI-generated models and **assets** for needed updates, based on the user scenario changes to improve customer journey and user behaviors. Analyst facilitates stakeholders in recommending changes. Analyst and dev team model the changes with use of AI development tools.
Analyst may help with testing, facilitating UAT testing, and implementation details.	Analyst analyzes AI-created test scenarios and edits for context and business need.
Analyst answers dev team questions during development.	Analyst reviews results, if automated testing with team and stakeholders, and facilitates go-no-go decision.
Analyst usually moves on to another project.	Analyst monitors data of new solution to track **user behavior** metrics and adjusts as needed.
Duration: usually one month to three years depending on scope/size.	Duration: one day to one month depending on scope/size.

The organization and analyst working with an AI and business analysis first world gets a totally different result that is ridiculously faster, of a higher quality, and avoids a huge amount of delay, cost, and waste.

Tim's Story

> While providing consulting services, I remember an organization having a perceived need for a new finance system and budgeting 20 million dollars to replace the old one. This situation highlights the challenge that many organizations face, where the desire to adopt new and flashy technologies often overshadows the potential benefits of optimizing or reusing existing systems. Initially, there was an assumption that a new finance system was needed to centralize finance functions and support a new operating model.
>
> Providing business analysis as a service has often allowed me to view the bigger picture and, often, I see reuse overlooked. The first principle in the agile manifesto is to "satisfy the customer through the early and continuous delivery of valuable software."[1] If the software exists already, it may be the fastest way to satisfy the need.
>
> However, good business analysis revealed that there were over 30 areas for improvement in the current system, and the estimated costs of $500,000 would be significantly lower than the budget allocated for the replacement. This scenario emphasizes the importance of conducting thorough business analysis and evaluating existing resources holistically before committing to large-scale initiatives.
>
> It also underscores the significance of being agile and open to reusing or repurposing existing assets when they can meet the organization's needs effectively. The "shiny new toy" syndrome is a common challenge in technology and business decision-making.
>
> My story emphasizes how organizations can benefit from a more balanced approach that considers both the allure of new solutions and the potential value that can be derived from optimizing or reusing current assets. In the future, organizations will need to create a culture that encourages critical evaluation, continuous improvement, and the efficient use of resources. This includes recognizing the value of what is already in place and being willing to invest in enhancements and optimizations rather than always opting for a complete system replacement.

Two important concepts that fit in with continuous improvement are *speed* and *pace*. While some organizations think delivery speed is most important, we think the concept of delivery pace or cadence is critical. An organization that finds the sweet spot of pace that can be maintained over a long period of time will reap the benefits. Pace is about maintaining a high rate of change over a sustained timeframe without losing enthusiasm and energy.

1. https://www.agilealliance.org/agile101/12-principles-behind-the-agile-manifesto/

Speed

Speed can be defined as how fast something moves.[1]

Teams leveraging GenAI will have speed on their side as they are able to

- leverage data analytics to prioritize and determine what to fix, change, and build,

- define increments of value much faster,

- identify and collaborate on user stories and acceptance criteria faster,

- model and prototype changes and solutions faster,

- setup test automation, and

- auto-generate initial drafts of documentation.

Pace

Pace can be defined as the speed at which someone or something moves, or with which something happens or changes.[2]

While speed and pace are similar in concept there is an important difference: pace is about maintaining speed over time, and is key for large organizational change. Speed is the distance covered over a period of given time. Pace is the speed at which something happens or changes; a consistent pace of change may vary the speed, either increasing or decreasing.

While speed can easily be achieved within a startup, once an organization becomes a medium or large entity, then speed can be counterproductive or damaging. Larger organizations require pace rather than speed. Pace is about knowing what value to deliver over acceptable time.

Pace allows a complex, large organization to consume change in a robust and stable manner. Too much speed in complex organizations will create multiple user behavior changes, meaning that data analysis cultivated from the changes is likely to result in conflicting information, stalling decision-making. Pace enables making hypotheses and experiments with stability, controlling changes, and enabling the organization to stay in front of its competitors.

An example is a drill bit. A small bit needs speed; however, the larger the bit, the less speed is needed, and too much can overheat the bit. Another practical example is any distance running

1. https://dictionary.cambridge.org/dictionary/english/speed

2. https://dictionary.cambridge.org/dictionary/english/pace

event. For a marathon, pace is important to win, and too much speed early on can be damaging. Even a 400-meter running race with too much speed early on can be a disadvantage at the 300-meter mark because someone who has paced themselves better may be faster to the finish line.

> "Agile management is about working smarter rather than harder. It's not about doing more work in less time: It's about generating more value from less work."[1]

An Example of Continued and Expanded Scope

Next, let's look at what this looks like for a new project/product/service rather than an update to an existing one.

As an example, let us say that the new project is implementing a process and technology to care for patients using biometrics from personal devices, and other data sources, to better predict who needs proactive care, diagnostic tests, and to send wellness reminders.

First, let's look at what may commonly be happening in many organizations. For many, the request and implementation process may resemble the following steps:

1. The IT and business leaders meet and decide to split this "program" into multiple projects, which are
   - one for the data collection interface from the patient's personal devices,
   - another for combining the patient data with other big data on biometrics,
   - a project for the deep-learning algorithm for predicting diagnostics,
   - a project for the deep-learning algorithm for proactive care plans, and
   - a project for the deep-learning algorithm for sending wellness reminders.
2. Once prioritized, each project would get assigned to a project manager or scrum team, perhaps.
3. A business analyst might be assigned to "write requirements" for each project.
4. The team and stakeholders pressure the analysts to get requirements done fast so that coding can start.
5. The projects are managed based on scope, schedule, and budget, which are defined without much analysis.
6. The team spends 40% of their time managing dependencies between the five teams and projects.
7. The team is plagued with "resource availability issues."
8. The risks on each project are managed in a "risk register," but the real risk of the actual data and user value coming together is thought of as "too hard" to manage.

1. Denning, S., The Age of Agile: How Smart Companies Are Transforming the Way Work Gets Done. AMACOM. 2018.

9. When the projects are implemented on schedule, budget, and scope, the team celebrates.

10. The business and external users become frustrated as the new solution pushes issues to other users, is annoying to patients, the calls increase to the nurses' desk that are not focused on patient care, patients are frustrated with messages that are not meaningful, patients are getting duplicate appointments and calls, and they feel like their overall care has actually gotten worse.

11. The business and users submit request after request to fix little aspects of the solution that get implemented one by one, creating an even bigger mess.

An "agile" way of working this same program would have looked like this:

1. Scrum, Scaled Agile Framework (SAFe), or other "agile" teams are deployed for each defined project.

2. There is a product owner for each "project team," a release train engineer (RTE) for each release train for SAFe teams.

3. Business analysts might be on these teams to write user stories.

4. The "front end teams" wait for the data teams to finish the data and AI work to connect to. Other managers fight over idle resources, while this team fights to hold on while they wait for the data team.

5. The teams are not coordinated in their sprint goals or release trains, and if they are using SAFe value streams to help, they are not defining their value streams correctly in a way that actually enables the use of the framework to get good results.

6. The team spends 40% of their time managing dependencies between the five teams and projects.

7. The team is plagued with "resource availability issues."

8. The business and external users become frustrated as the new solution pushes issues to other users, is annoying to patients, the calls increase to the nurses' desk that are not focused on patient care, patients are frustrated with messages that are not meaningful, patients are getting duplicate appointments and calls, and they feel like their overall care has actually gotten worse.

9. The business and users submit request after request to fix little aspects of the solution that get implemented one by one, creating an even bigger mess.

A newer way of working, with the **AI Analysis Accelerator Framework**, an AI and business analysis-first mentality, would look like this:

1. The skilled business analyst responsible for this new value stream and customer journey is assigned to this effort. They work with leadership to define a product vision that includes the **business results** and **user behavior changes** defined from a patient and customer point of view. Things like
    - patient health outcomes that achieve a higher value score (**business results**),
    - cost efficiencies are realized for achieving patient outcomes; most cost reductions will be in patient scheduling (**business results**),
    - patients are engaging with the reminders, have proactive care, and data collection is from their devices (**user behavior changes**),
    - patients that used to get behind in preventive care are more up to date, making and keeping appointments (**user behavior changes**),
    - nurses and doctors' time is used more on patient care and less on admin (**user behavior changes**), and
    - doctors are able to diagnose critical issues earlier than before due to improved, timely data (**user behavior changes**).

2. The business analyst works with the leaders and team to form a **hypothesis** that will guide the team. It ends up being something like this:

    > *We believe that if we can leverage data AI and GenAI to help patients leverage their biomarkers and other biomarker data, we can create proactive scheduling throughout the health journey to improve health outcomes for patients.*

3. The business analyst meets with the team and stakeholders to review the existing customer journey maps, reviewing the critical patient/user interaction points, such as
    - setting up the data collection on their device, and giving permissions,
    - configuring the settings for how often and what messages they get back,
    - having patients make appointments with conversational AI-based chatbots who recommend and book appointment times and the clinician,
    - answering patient questions based on biomarkers (AI driven),
    - answering patient questions from the doctors (talk or text AI),
    - having doctors view and respond to data-based alerts,
    - having nurses and clinicians respond to patient chats,
    - having clinicians look at an overview of patient data, which helps see the big picture, history, and chats; clinicians can have a chat with an AI tool to ask questions about the patient and their charts, data, and history,
    - having doctors use AI to help with diagnosis and treatment pathways, and
    - having AI interpret conversations, and then code the appointment for the doctor, sending a confirmation to them.

4. The business analyst leads the team in identifying the highest-risk **user behavior change** and the highest risk item on the list that poor data quality would compromise.

5. The analyst helps the team to define lean **experiments** that they need to do before building and deploying. They identify the following initial **experiment** based on the user change risk and data quality risk:

   - A lean **experiment** to build a working prototype and work with a self-selected group of patients on the setup and collection of data from their devices. The team is looking to learn the following:
     - What are the users thinking and feeling when setting up their devices?
     - What makes a patient hesitant to stop the process and not allow permission to use their data?
     - What data are the patients comfortable sharing for medical purposes?
   - The analyst uses GenAI to create the test cases against the value streams, customer journeys, and the automation of the test cases, but still has a HUGELY important task of validating that these are the right tests to run and automate to make the organization's outcomes a reality.

6. The lean **experiments** and learnings from them guide the analyst and team to discuss with the business leaders what the best path forward is.

7. This is all built quickly with GenAI and is ready to implement quite fast. The communications, decisions, and strategy on **experiments** and order to build, and the deployment strategy of the prototype, is far more important.

8. The analyst sets up usage monitoring and continues to monitor the process performance as the team works, deploys, etc.

9. The team, with the analyst's good practices, can not only see evidential data of the process working, but how each scenario and its variations are performing.

The AI Analysis Accelerator Framework and How the Concepts Fit Together

The picture below shows the relationships between the **AI Analysis Accelerator Framework** concepts. Each concept in the framework has a unique relationship to other concepts. Together, the concepts align the business results to the team tasks and activities being done through analysis to complete the concepts between them.

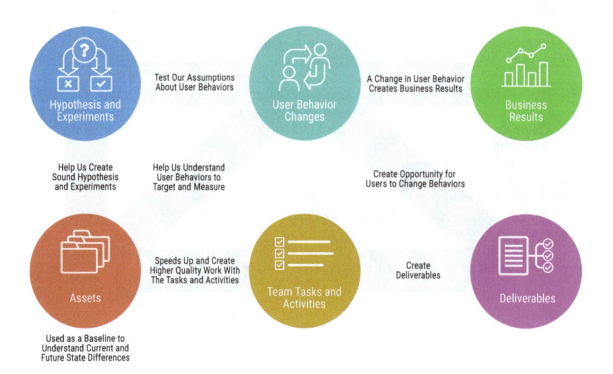

Hypothesis and Experiments

Help Us Create
Sound Hypothesis
and Experiments

Assets

Used as a Baseline to
Understand Current and
Future State Differences

Start here … though **assets** may provide information to create, confirm, or change a **hypothesis**.

Things like:

- Metrics/Data on process/user performance
- User Journey Maps
- Value Stream Maps
- Process Models
- Data Flow Diagrams
- Business Rules Defined
- State Transition Diagrams

Every effort (project, product, enhancement, defect, fix, process change … has a **hypothesis** to work on …

Every effort benefits from analysis **assets**, or else, you are gambling on short term working memory of stakeholders and the team to drive alignment.

This does not work. It only creates rework.

When Analysis is Set Up to be Incomplete

Many teams today have business analysts assigned at the component level, or application level. This has never been a model that strengthens analysis practices because these components or applications are only a small part of a value stream and customer journey. So, what happens when we try to analyze by component when AI automatically writes that code? We optimize for something that no longer provides the value. The full end-to-end analysis provides value; we cannot give tech solutions to analysts, and analysts cannot accept them from leaders as success will not be realized. The full picture must be looked at, and now it can be, with far less effort, higher accuracy, more value but also a far more skilled and analysis-based approach.

Descriptive and predictive data analysis using AI will help analysts develop **hypotheses** that will enable detailed and lean **experiments** to be performed to enable sophisticated decision-making. An example might be predictive data projection on life expectancy by changing specific daily habits—increasing good habits and reducing bad habits.

Prescriptive analytics will advise on what to do about the predictions. We need to fundamentally rethink how we use data, and analysts are at the forefront of helping business leaders at all levels rethink their ideas to leverage data and AI.

These analytics are already in many organizations, and as AI advances, these get better, more data and knowledge are available to leverage in them, and the manner in which we access them improves and becomes easier.

Paradigm Shifts for Continuous Analysis

Paradigm Shift—Enabling Analysis to Focus on Value

 For existing processes, the paradigm shifts from a backlog of requests to perform research, investigate, elicit, and analyze, to a dashboard of data analytics showing us how the value steams and customer journeys are performing, with recommendations on what updates should be made to improve it.

For new processes, the elicitation should focus on defining the metrics, value stream, and customer journey; not on asking what the requirements are, as the requirements are embedded in the business flow.

> Many of us would say, asking "what are the requirements?" has never been a good practice, yet the majority of organizations fall into this pattern and perform requirements elicitation and analysis this way!

The emerging new world is showing us that our ideas as humans can't possibly determine the requirements at a granular level at speed. We need the help of AI to determine them, and a new process to leverage the possibilities, interconnections, dependencies, and data.

Using a "request-driven backlog process" is no longer a sufficient way to make the most of our resources, to improve customer experiences and operational efficiencies. Using a "request-driven backlog process" will only slow down the organization in making needed adaptations to processes and put it at risk as others move much faster.

Paradigm Shift—Continuously Monitoring Value and Updating Analysis Models and Metrics

In this new world, imagine a business analyst, product owner, or product manager logging into a dashboard to view a product's value stream. They will see how the value stream is performing, and what improvements are recommended.

Then, they evaluate the data for potential quality issues and use analysis techniques to validate the issue, research and model the recommended changes, run some automated impact analysis, collaborate with peers and leaders on a summary of this information, and make a decision (daily) on what to change. Then they determine whether an A/B test is needed, approve the changes, and track the data again the next day.

All the code needed to make the update is automatically done with the use of AI, and regression tests are also automated, of course.

Paradigm Shift—Continuous Discovery and Exploration

For many teams, discovery has been a phase where, once an idea or issue was prioritized, a discovery phase was planned for. Now, discovery and exploration will no longer be based on a backlog of requests to prioritize and look at, or a phase at all.

AI will do much of the opportunity and problem identification for us, quantifying those items for us, and recommending solutions. Sure, there will be other ideas and things that people will identify that need to be looked at, but discovery as we know it will fundamentally change in order to leverage AI and reduce the time it takes to get from idea to implementation.

Implementation of possible solutions will be fed to us by AI, and A/B will be tested as discovery. Does this mean we can accelerate the path from idea to implementation without all the discovery sessions and workshops? Sort of. There will always be a place for workshop-style collaboration, but it will have different triggers, inputs, and purposes.

Imagine a middle manager has an idea for a new feature for an internal business process/system, or an external-facing product. This manager would traditionally submit the idea, then it would be put through some sort of combination of prioritization and socialization, where politics, relationships, and agendas determine whether it gets prioritized and worked on. The team would be assigned and some discovery and analysis would happen to determine the scope, requirements, design, and get to development, testing, and implementation. It would be months and sometimes years before the idea is realized.

AI will provide the capability to erase most of the politics of this by giving us objective and evidence-based data about what processes and user enablement actions need to be addressed. AI will identify and model some potential solutions.

AI still needs validation, where the same analysis skills, scenario identification, end-to-end test modeling, and collaboration with various partners on impacts and change management are necessary.

Discovery will have a lot more to do with analyzing and validating impact, and redefining the measurements and monitoring where needed, than discovering requirements.

In some ways, discovery as we currently know it may have a place in brand-new product development, yet by the time a discovery workshop or process is planned, AI could have coded something to be validated, tested, and refined.

What this comes down to is continuous discovery—a process that is less about ideas and issues reported and is more about proactive monitoring while matching AI-identified issues and opportunities with strategic conversations and reports from various business units and customers. Matching where all of this is telling a story and validating and testing potential solutions; discovering what solutions might model best to solve more angles of the same problem or opportunity being identified from many places.

In theory, this should be happening today, but for many organizations this is too time-consuming, so many do not do it.

Continuous discovery and analysis are important pieces of making AI work well and efficiently in changing value streams and getting **business results**. But, what does this really look like?

Requirements, ideas, defects, enhancements, and changes come from so many places. *All* requirements are existing products and processes or are part of a theorized change that is needed. They are based on an understanding of the current state, and an idea of what the future state might be. It is a **hypothesis** that we believe that changing the current state will create new **user behaviors** that, in turn, will create **business results**.

Continuous discovery, research, data insights, monitoring of key measurements, and connecting the dots—all of this is pointing to the need to act, **hypothesize, and experiment** to get the right changes implemented, and fast, with help from AI.

Keeping continuous discovery as a practice enables pace and agility. Continuous discovery through analysis and collaboration with the help of AI is what will enable change and quality change to happen in a complex, speed-driven environment.

When every business and customer process is continuously measured and monitored—giving leaders and analysts the data they need to detect performance issues before they become costly—we have true agility and adaptability to improve the processes and compete.

Each customer journey has an owner, who also has an analyst, and together they analyze and make decisions based on continuous discovery, monitoring, and exploration. They work with adjacent customer journeys, whose owners and analysts collaborate to share data, on running experiments, and they see the impact one another's processes have on each other.

Paradigm Shift—Continuous Experimentation

 Many organizations, as they have matured through their software development, have embodied experimentation as a way of working. Organizations with external-facing products tend to be more experienced at running experiments, and organizations with more traditional products (physical or services, not software as the product), are starting to see experiments as a technique to manage complexity.

Analysis and product management are coming closer and closer together as traditional organizations that used to build software for internal users then started using software to interact with customers. Now, through digital transformations, they find themselves developing systems that are critical for customers and internal employees to use as a competitive advantage to service their non-software products. So, as more and more systems become external facing, the stakes are higher for the value stream, customer journey, and data to be used and measured.

Continuous experimentation is the future, and mature teams are already embodying this. With AI, this will only grow in importance, and it will be lightning fast for AI-driven organizations.

Business analysis skills will be needed to constantly test and experiment with models. So, what do we mean by models?

Imagine a team being able to define, run, and see the results of a code change in a matter of minutes. Or, how about being able to model various code changes and run them simultaneously against production to see which would perform best. Users get the current code, but you are able to see how four other versions might perform differently.

In order to do this, not only does the organization need to be AI enabled, and this will become easier and easier to become, but then the business analysis skills needed by any role executing this will be paramount.

Analysis skills will be needed to understand the business result, customer behavior changes, user actions, and how to instruct AI to change the right rules or journey and collaborate with technical team members to set up and review the results.

In the future, those in analysis roles will spend most of their time defining **experiments** and running experimental models to determine which solution to implement. They will still need all their relationship and facilitation skills as they will skillfully need to communicate and bring leaders and groups together to make decisions and discuss the **experiments** and findings.

In the future, analysis roles will create **assets** that are used and updated continuously as part of continuous analysis, rather than specifically approved for a single project. These **assets** are things like

- value stream high-level maps,
- customer journey maps,
- process models,
- impact maps,
- user scenarios,
- user groups,
- visual models (state transition diagrams, decision tables, workflows, scope models, data flow diagrams, and many more),
- data definitions and relationship models, and
- rule definitions and models.

What we are advocating is that the process architecture **assets** of an organization be defined, created, and managed—ongoing. AI tools can draft these **assets**, and they are now not as costly to create and maintain. Then they can be used to quickly make better decisions. This has always been true, but few organizations have invested in it. Yes, it has been expensive to do in the past. Now, this is imperative and less costly, while creating even more return on investment. These **assets** can be tied directly to code, enabling AI to do its work!

Business analysis is about helping organizations change. What blows our minds is thinking about the rate of change some organizations will be able to achieve when they have the analysis and AI intersections figured out and optimized.

For example, AI is capable of identifying the problems to be solved. AI is able to find these issues faster than humans. What is stopping us humans from setting up a process that allows AI to monitor key process measurements, and alerting us when there are problems, and how much it is costing the organization to let the problem continue?

Chapter Summary

- This chapter presents a future state where analysis is not confined to a specific point in time project, but is an ongoing, continuous process. It emphasizes the need to adopt a mindset of lean continuous improvement, ensuring that analysis is dynamic and responsive to the evolving business marketplace.

- The future state emphasizes the importance of enabling analysis to focus on value within a rapidly changing world.

- A fundamental aspect of analysis in the future state is **hypotheses and experimentation.** This chapter highlights the role of experimentation in driving innovation and adaptation, emphasizing its significance in shaping the analytical outcomes.

Action Items

- Start developing a mindset of continuous improvement within yourself and your organization, emphasizing that business analysis is an ongoing process rather than a phase. Encourage regular reviews and enhancements to your analysis practices, embracing change as a means of staying ahead in a fast-paced environment.
- Invest in maintaining core **assets**, value streams, and customer journeys that facilitate continuous discovery and exploration.
- **Experiment** with new ideas, methodologies, and technologies, while fostering a mindset of innovation within the business analysis process.

These action items aim to guide individuals and organizations in transitioning toward a future state where analysis is a continuous and dynamic activity, aligned with a culture of continuous improvement, value-focused discovery, and experimentation.

Future State—Analysis is NOT a Phase!

5 Business Analysis Roles in the Future

In this chapter we look at how business analysis is a "knowledge worker" role and how the practice is being elevated with AI-driven work. We look at how the **AI Analysis Accelerator Framework** can elevate the role, practice, analysis, and business results.

We will continue with more details and depth on the example of the medical clinic from Chapter 4, showing examples of a value stream map and customer journey maps aligned to strategic metrics. We will also bring all pieces of the **AI Analysis Accelerator Framework** together into a single view for the medical clinic example.

We will look at AI implications on business analysis deliverables. And we will look deeper at how the business analyst role—using the **AI Analysis Accelerator Framework**—can operate, and needs to operate, at a much more elevated, strategic level.

Vignette

Samantha Ghent

I'm excited this morning to meet with Strategic Lead Business Analyst, Kathy. She is showing me the latest dashboard she is working on for our new product suite. The vision is that, like other value streams and customer journeys, I, and other leaders, as well as the business analysis team, can see the performance of our products and services through the value streams, customer journeys, and user trends mapped to our strategy. It alerts us to variances we have defined and lets us know the cost, or opportunity cost, if variances need to be looked at.

This is where I love my job. I can see where the work we are doing is actually making a difference in the organization's strategy. We are part of the business, not a servicer, not a partner.

The Future Business Analyst

The business analysis roles of the future will be elevated in skills and filled with higher-value tasks than previously. Business analysis roles and skills will be much needed as AI stands to change just about every customer, user, business, and system process within each organization.

As AI takes hold in everything from how potential and existing customers interact with your organization, to how your internal processes and people interact with one another, and how systems interact, our roles will inevitably change.

Doing business analysis really well in the future will enable and demand that we take practices from many disciplines (such as those mentioned in Chapter 2—Lean, TQM, Six-Sigma, Agile, DevOps, and traditional software development frameworks) and weave a connected analysis practice that drives value to many parts of the organization.

Business Analysis is "Knowledge Work"

Analysis professionals do knowledge work; that is, non-routine problem-solving with a combination of analysis, relationships, abstraction, decomposition, creativity, and divergent and convergent thinking. AI will enable knowledge workers to be more creative, use evidence-based data, and solve more complex problems that have many dependencies. This will require knowledge workers to see their role more broadly and as able to tackle problem sets that previously have been unimaginable. Analysis is required across the breadth of a value stream and customer journey, including all **team tasks and activities** required to deliver a product or service. Knowledge workers will need to have highly developed skills to work across this wide platform.

Business analysis roles are the quintessential knowledge workers. They use a combination of user, business, and system information to solve problems and leverage opportunities to get to better organizational outcomes. They must do this within a changing environment, changing the ecosystem of internal and external factors, all while balancing human and analytical factors.

Business analysis roles must "practice" their work—nothing is a repeatable procedure.

AI is Changing the "Knowledge Worker" and Business Analysis

AI will enable many of today's problems to be solved quite easily, leaving the connection to a bigger context and larger problem space open and ripe for innovation.

Imagine being able to have AI process an amount of information that would bog down our own limitations of working memory. We see this already with AI assisting medical practitioners with diagnoses. AI can process more patterns and data than humanly possible and bring up questions that would take much longer for any human brain to get to.

In business analysis, this knowledge base is akin to seeing a larger ecosystem, think 300 business analysts on a huge program sharing information and patterns from their respective parts and pieces of projects, systems, and programs. We are not advocating for one business analyst in the future for every 300 of the past; rather, think about the improvements that could be made when an analysis professional has this much more processing capacity at their fingertips to solve problems with. The same is true for developers and other roles as well.

A Larger Ecosystem—Back to our Example

In Chapter 4 we looked at the example of a medical clinic. Let's continue using this context and look at being AI enabled, but without a new way of doing analysis! In the old way of doing analysis

- tech and business leaders thought about ways of using new technology and ways to solve problems, and started matching tech to problems,

- they funded projects,

- they assigned an analyst to do the analysis, and

- after implementation, the leaders kept requesting tasks and enhancements to get everything to perform better, and those requests competed with other shiny ideas.

Now, in a medical clinic, they might implement a backlog that looks something like this:

- Enable GenAI to dictate clinician notes during patient appointments, saving the practitioners time in writing notes.

- Enable GenAI to interpret clinician notes and assign medical codes for health records and billing purposes.

- Enable GenAI to chat with patients about symptom reporting, questions between appointments, appointment scheduling, lab results, appointment prep, and follow-up conversations.

- Enable deep-learning AI to detect, when possible, conditions that match, and let the doctor know there is a potential symptom/biomarker/diagnosis fit to consider.

The current way of working in many organizations would be to make each of these a project, and then assign a business analyst and a team to them. The scope of analysis is often limited to the scope of the project, and, in some organizations, this means limited to the scope of IT, or a single application team in IT. The solution has already been ideated, and the problem we are looking to solve is somewhat identified, but isolated. The measurements seem to be about clinician productivity. The assumption here is that productivity equates to or leads to better patient care and more time for the patients.

As these projects are implemented, however, customer service gets more escalated chats to respond to, patients start leaving the practice, and anecdotal evidence shows that patients are frustrated with the quality of care and lack of coordination; they don't feel seen and heard. All the capabilities of AI and tech are implemented and used, so what's wrong? Leaders are confused as clinicians are reporting more time with patients, and more productivity. The projects were all successful, on schedule, and on budget, for the most part.

So, what went wrong?

It turns out that, upon further research, patients did not feel like anything was coordinated, the information they provided was not used in consideration of the responses they got back, they felt like they had to continue to explain things at every interaction, and they grew frustrated at a what seemed like uncoordinated attempt to provide medical care.

The larger ecosystem and "knowledge work" was not part of the analysis work, or not enough. The value streams, customer journeys, and metrics of success were not defined well, and patients ended up being disappointed and leaving. The real metrics that mattered—business analysis seeing the end-to-end value stream, customer journey, and how technology enabled the actual value being delivered—was missing.

Now, let's look at how this could be different.

Take a look at the following visual of our **AI Analysis Accelerator Framework** in action.

| Assets | Hypothesis and Experiments | Team Tasks and Activities | Deliverables | User Behavior Changes | Business Results |

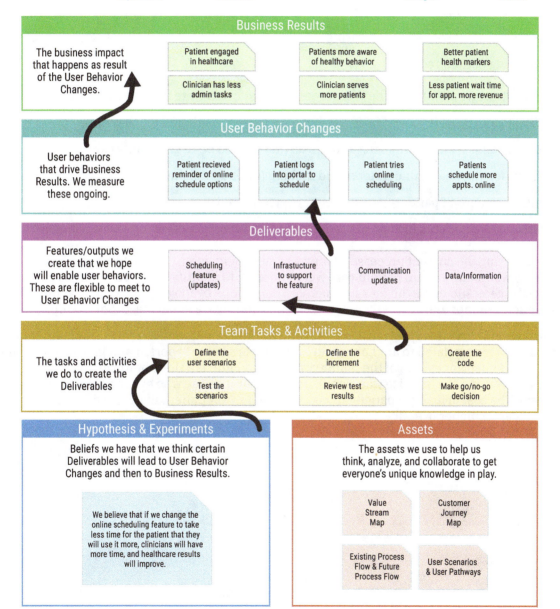

Business Results

The business impact that happens as result of the User Behavior Changes.

- Patient engaged in healthcare
- Patients more aware of healthy behavior
- Better patient health markers
- Clinician has less admin tasks
- Clinician serves more patients
- Less patient wait time for appt. more revenue

User Behavior Changes

User behaviors that drive Business Results. We measure these ongoing.

- Patient recieved reminder of online schedule options
- Patient logs into portal to schedule
- Patient tries online scheduling
- Patients schedule more appts. online

Deliverables

Features/outputs we create that we hope will enable user behaviors. These are flexible to meet to User Behavior Changes

- Scheduling feature (updates)
- Infrastucture to support the feature
- Communication updates
- Data/Information

Team Tasks & Activities

The tasks and activities we do to create the Deliverables

- Define the user scenarios
- Define the increment
- Create the code
- Test the scenarios
- Review test results
- Make go/no-go decision

Hypothesis & Experiments

Beliefs we have that we think certain Deliverables will lead to User Behavior Changes and then to Business Results.

We believe that if we change the online scheduling feature to take less time for the patient that they will use it more, clinicians will have more time, and healthcare results will improve.

Assets

The assets we use to help us think, analyze, and collaborate to get everyone's unique knowledge in play.

- Value Stream Map
- Customer Journey Map
- Existing Process Flow & Future Process Flow
- User Scenarios & User Pathways

A Larger Ecosystem—Back to our Example

Instead of taking a backlog of technical ideas to implement, the analysis process defined the value streams and customer journeys as

- scheduling an appointment,
- patient diagnosis and action plan,
- patient treatment,
- proactive patient care and monitoring, and
- monitoring patient recovery.

Then, with strategic alignment, the measurements of success were defined as

- getting to an accurate diagnosis faster, but with more meaningful touch points,
- patients being seen by clinicians as often as they should be to get quality care,
- patients feeling heard, understood, and making fewer complaints,
- health outcomes of patients getting better overtime, and
- referrals from patients bringing in their friends and family increasing service demand.

Upon measuring the current processes, using AI and data insights, the analyst and team could see exactly where the gaps in patient care were and start to identify where AI might be able to improve the gaps and move the measurements. This is done by looking holistically at the value stream and customer journey, rather than an idea to optimize a small piece. For example:

- Analysis may find that, previously, an isolated AI implementation to reduce clinician time taking notes correlated to an increase in billing errors being reported and investigated. The cost was still lower overall of the billing process and clinician time; however, the rate of patients leaving the practice was significantly higher in those who experienced the billing errors. The cost of losing a patient and establishing a new patient in the practice is significantly higher overall.

- Analysis may find that the GenAI chatbot implementation, which was intended to reduce customer service costs and increase responsiveness to patients, led to missed information to help diagnosis, and frustrated patients. Patients were chatting not knowing if it was a chatbot or human, and they were reporting symptoms that were never being seen or analyzed by a clinician or an AI process that tracks symptoms. The chatbot was also asking questions of the patients that were not making sense or were repeating questions already addressed. Frustrated patients, missed data signals, and uncoordinated patient communications led to an increase in scheduled appointments, increased escalations of chat messages, and frustrated patients feeling confused and leaving the practice. These are not the results the organization intended on getting. Often this happens when an isolated idea was not looked at in a bigger context, and not using data to track and investigate the value stream and metric alignment. This paints a very different picture of how to use AI; it can be easy to implement the wrong thing, costing the organization dearly.

- Analysis here might lead to experimenting with AI to track patient tone and frustration earlier, or to looking for symptoms in the chats and alerting a doctor to take a more holistic review and proactive communication process with patients.

Knowledge Work Enables Strategic Alignment Facilitation

With the appropriate strategic alignment comes better prioritization and a view of ideas that is more holistic, optimizing the entire system of value rather than a single process or metric.

When we can transparently see the linkage from the organization's strategy to the **business results**, to the metrics and outcomes that look at the desired behaviors for success, we can more seamlessly align the work we do (the outputs, **deliverables**, and **team tasks and activities**).

Without this alignment, most teams are grasping for features based on opinion, previous work experience, or what they can build consensus on, but these features may not actually align strategically. This creates a team working straight from strategy to **deliverables** with no real alignment between multiple teams and the work they all do. If this seems unlikely, think again. It is the norm for most organizations, and we have seen very few get this right! Most organizations take a strategy, and each senior executive sets their own goals against it, crafts their own deliverable plan to meet their own metrics, which drives their own bonus pay structure. They present their plans to one another in the senior executive circle, tweaking things to "work together" on strategic alignment. But, along the way, the real outcomes are not measured until well after the idea was committed to, if at all. What is left are disappointed customers, users, and shareholders.

Analysis is truly aligning the strategic intent to the work, and the advances in GenAI and data analytics are helping us do this even better. By letting us have easier access to the data, we can align a well-crafted and measurable strategy to the work being done, and track and monitor the results as we work.

Without this analysis, ideas will be generated and considered at all levels to optimize what that person needs for their organization, rather than the organization's performance overall, often shifting cost and issues from one part to another.

Facilitating Faster Alignment of Strategic Imperatives with Technology

Getting the data and metrics set up is critical to this analysis strategy. This allows for evidence-based decision-making and not allowing teams to determine their own goals based on what they are confident they can deliver, but which may not actually align to strategic intent other than in a fancy presentation to everyone "showing" alignment.

Having outcome-based metrics, and measuring the aligned user behaviors as we build, is the only way to dynamically change and prioritize.

Back to our example of an online medical appointment booking system. Let's dig into how a team would align to strategic intent and measure as they work to dynamically prioritize and change course as needed, leveraging AI.

The skilled business analyst responsible for this new value stream and customer journey is assigned to this effort.

The value stream map below shows the high-level process of the medical appointment:

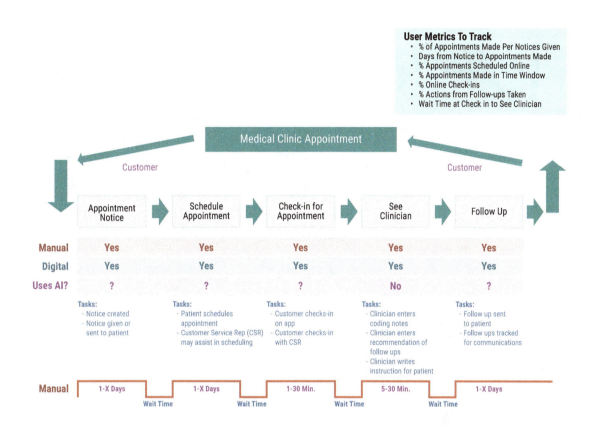

The following two customer journey maps show, first, the high-level journey for a medical appointment and, second, a more detailed one for the scheduling of the appointment.

High-level medical appointment customer journey map:

Patient					
Medical Appointment	Determine Appointment Need	Schedule Appointment	Check-in for Appointment	See Clinician	Follow Up
Customer Goals	- Understand urgency - Understand cost - Find a clinican	- Find time slot when I am available - Find time within recommended interval	- Quickly check in - Not wait long	- Get answers - Get diagnosis - Get next steps	- Understand next steps - Understand urgency of next steps
Touchpoints	- Recieve notice	- Online schedule - Call for appointment	- Check-in in person - Check-in at kiosk - Check-in on app - Wait to be called	- Talk to clinician - Testing	- Papers from appointment - Email - Phone call - Text message
Customer Commentary	- Ugh another appointment!	- This takes too much time	- That was easy! - I don't want to wait too long	- Anxious - Nervous	- More To-Dos - I don't want to - Will this work?
Customer Experience	😐	☹️	🙂	☹️	😐	☹️
Opportunities	- Provide convenient options - Predict when they need to be seen	- Make it faster and easier	- Reduce wait time with better scheduling optimization	- Reduce anxiety with better prep info for appointment	- Easy app checklists - Bio monitoriing - Automated reminders and nudges

Business Analysis Roles in the Future

A more detailed customer journey map for scheduling an appointment:

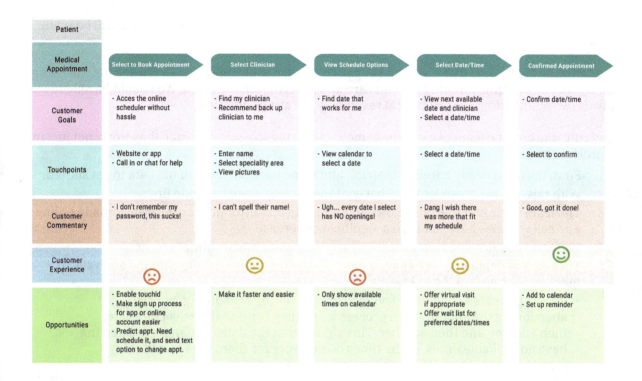

The team works with leadership to define a product vision that includes the **business result** and **user behavior changes** defined from a patient and customer point of view. Things like

- patient health outcomes are better and improve **(business result)**,

- cost efficiencies in serving patients, lots of overhead costs to schedule are reduced **(business result)** by
    - patients are using the online scheduling **(user behavior changes)**, and
    - patients are calling less to schedule **(user behavior changes)**.

Remember from the last chapter that our **business result** is the way we align results with the strategic intent—patient care and lower costs through efficiencies. Then, with these outcome measurements (all 100% about behaviors of users), we have measurements of the patient behaviors. When patients successfully use the online scheduling, then fewer calls will be made to schedule.

Hypothesis: We believe that if we can get patients to schedule online, then fewer calls will come in, freeing up our time for other patient care and lowering costs overall. We should be able to divert two administration staff to $1M revenue-generating activities.

Let's dig into how the team can use these metrics and the **hypothesis** while they work, not just in a project charter:

1. First, the team needs baseline metrics, and some basic analysis of the data to get started.
2. With this, the team can look at what goal/metric they want to tackle first.
3. The team finds that the data shows about 15% of appointments are currently made online, and call volumes have not seen a significant decrease.
4. The team decides to go after the "% of appointments made online" metric.
5. They look at detailed user behavior data, leveraging GenAI to help with the analysis. In quick time, they find the following:
   - 40% of patients are actually trying to use the online scheduling, but are abandoning the appointment process when they continually select one date, then another, and then another. This signals that the dates patients are selecting have no available times, or the times do not work for them. The team brain storms ideas to solve this problem and come up with:
     - have a "first available option,"
     - have a "first available for my preferred doctor" option, and
     - have a "first available for my schedule" option, where the patient can select the days of the week and three time slots that would work for them.
6. Using the existing value stream, GenAI is able to write up these user stories and acceptance criteria (A/C), so the team edits these user stories and A/C.
7. The team plans to work them in this same order.
8. The team works on the "first available" option, releases it, and monitors the patients' behavior. Numbers get better!
9. Talking to the front desk, they hear anecdotes that patients are calling wanting their own doctor, not just any first available. Great, that is what we are working on next!
10. They release the "first available for my preferred doctor," and watch the data. Wow, it is moving in the right direction again, and getting better. Within a few weeks, the team sees the 40% marker happen! Calls also have a noticeable decrease.
11. Now leadership is excited and wants that 40% to become 80%!

12. Leaders meet with the team, and a coordinated plan is put together to help educate patients about the new online scheduling features. Besides communications when interacting with patients in the office, the team brainstorms, with the help of GenAI, the following:
    - Add an on-hold message for those who call in that they can schedule online.
    - Email and text proactive reminders of appointments that need to be scheduled and provide a link to schedule online.
    - Add a link to the medical records and dashboard views for patients to remind them, and create easy access to the online scheduler.
13. The team meets to prioritize which they think will move the needle most. GenAI writes the user stories and A/C, the team (stakeholders, PO, dev team, and business analyst may all be included) edits them.
14. The team implements one and measures the patient behavior... And this approach repeats itself.

Facilitate Constant Prioritization

The example above demonstrates constant prioritization and adaptive work based on evidence-based, user-behavior-focused outcomes. As teams make their journey to becoming AI-enabled organizations, they will struggle with constant prioritization. This will force them to truly define what their success metrics—**user behavior changes** metrics aligned to **business results**— are and align work items to these metrics. It will also start to force organizations to measure project progress to metrics as they deploy and cut projects that are not delivering on those metrics as teams progress in incremental progress, measuring as they work.

The team is allowing the data and AI to help them dynamically facilitate priorities with the foundation of behavior-driven and strategically aligned metrics.

Analysis Levels of Detail

Analysis can be thought of in three horizons as defined by IIBA's Agile Extension to BABOK Guide®[1]. The three horizons are:

- Strategy

- Initiative

- Delivery

1. International Institute of Business Analysis and Agile Alliance. Agile Extension to the BABOK® Guide, v. 2. International Institute of Business Analysis. 2018.

These are three different levels of detail in which to view the analysis work. These horizons will likely transition to become one single horizon as AI automates the initiative and delivery horizons. The strategic horizon will become the key horizon as eventually automation will link it directly to continuous delivery. So much emphasis will be placed on the strategic horizon as this will be the epicenter in big thinking, prioritizing, and working on strategic decisions. Quick, initial **experiment** cycles will induce immediate monitoring of value stream and product performance. A cycle of continuous improvement will start faster than most can currently imagine. The lines between strategy, initiative, and delivery will blur as a focus on continuous improvement takes over "project" and "initiative" thinking.

Strategic initiative will focus on answering the questions:

- What are the big efforts to undertake?
- What are our guiding values, assumptions, and **hypotheses**?
- What have we learned that changes or influences our strategy?
- What can we do to reduce risk and **experiment** to learn more?

If we think things are complex and changing fast today, we are about to see an entire other level of change and complexity.

Business Analysis in the Future

Assets   Hypothesis and Experiments   Team Tasks and Activities   Deliverables   User Behavior Changes   Business Results

In the future, **assets** will be the platform for change. AI will orchestrate the value streams, customer journeys, rules, and data quickly at scale, essentially the business architecture. Business analysis will utilize these **assets** for analyzing improvement changes and facilitating decision-making with leaders and stakeholders. Continuous improvement will mean these **assets** will evolve and be updated through each initiative, small or large.

The analyst will review data using existing **assets** to develop a **hypothesis** to maximize **business results**. This will then form the basis for **experiments** to validate the theories for putting them into business operations.

To measure the change, it will be necessary for the analyst to work with stakeholders to develop accurate **user behavior changes**. Our job, as business analysis practitioners, is to align software features to increase changes in customer behavior. Our work will be honed to only delivering those software changes that positively influence customer behavior, to gain the best result for the organization.

Team tasks and activities will focus on fast demos and prototypes with codeless apps, where the business teams and analysts will model future option scenarios with descriptive and predictive data, evaluating test scenarios and making updates. Each team task should be traced backwards to changes in user customer behavior.

The business analyst's **deliverables** will look totally different to current ones. No longer will user stories be necessary to write good code. Value streams, customer journeys, rules, and data will be enough for AI to deliver working software. In the future, analysts will construct prototypes, **experiments**, and code sets in test environments and live, automated test results and predictive value stream performance data.

Business results are the final measure of success. Analysts will be involved in tracing user behavior to measurements in financial results of revenue and expense.

AI Implications on Traditional Business Analysis Deliverables

We have already shown how AI can create pretty much all of the most common business analysis **deliverables**. This will continue to advance, evolve, and get to a point where the quality is very good, and integrated into our processes as a normal thing. However, this does not mean business analysis is no longer needed. Strong business analysis skills are still needed to determine the trust level needed and ensure that the AI-generated analysis is correct and usable to get the needed results.

Below we look at the traditional business analysis **deliverables**, how AI is impacting them, and as we step into using AI more, what still needs to happen.

Traditional Deliverable	AI Implications	Stepping into Leveraging AI
Requirements/spec document	AI can write the system documentation for us based on reading the code, and write the spec from the code that has been written. The documentation will be written in whatever format or level of detail we prompt it to write at, and for whichever audience we would like. BAs will need to be skilled in prompting AI to get the results that they need. BAs will not be able to prompt effectively without solid business analysis skills.	We rethink what a spec doc or requirements doc is, who it is for, and why we are creating it. Many are finding and will find that they are no longer needed. Some teams may find a reason or audience for a document or a record of documentation, and AI will do most of the work.
User stories and acceptance criteria	AI tools write user stories and acceptance criteria and are getting really good at writing them. BAs will be needed to prompt the AI agent effectively with user story skills as input to the prompting. BAs will need to also understand and be skilled in user stories and acceptance criteria in order to work with the AI to get the right user stories and the right level of quality and context.	Is writing them the goal? No. The conversation that is inspired amongst the stakeholders and team is what this is all about. It's not about the writing of them, it's about the conversation and shared understanding. Analysts play a critical role in facilitating this shared understanding with special skills in structured conversations, critical thinking, and user scenario identification.

Business Analysis Roles in the Future

Traditional Deliverable	AI Implications	Stepping into Leveraging AI
Visual models (process models, state diagrams, decision tables, etc.)	AI tools can generate visual models that analysts have typically created and can create them based on code, a description, or a prompt. BAs will need to deeply understand the visual models to know when to use them, how to prompt for them, and how to interpret and edit them to the context of the work.	Analysts will still need to edit them to the goals and audience they are collaborating with, to make them valuable for deep and productive conversations. Again, the model isn't about the documentation; it's about the conversation they inspire with the help of an analyst trained in how to use the models to guide the right conversations with the right people.
Decision logic	AI can create this from a prompt or from reading existing code. AI can even analyze for gaps, duplicates, etc. BAs can leverage this, and will also need to understand the decision logic and business goals well enough to make the logic even better for the business context and goals.	Analysts will need to validate and analyze the scenarios that apply for their context, and edit them, then connect to other **assets**, scenarios, and conversations.
Screen Mock-ups	AI can design these given the right prompts and inputs. BAs will need to learn to provide the right prompts and inputs.	Analysts will need to facilitate the decision between AI generated designs, analyzing the various designs and fit to culture, style, and strategy of the organization.
Test scenarios and plans	AI can identify these from common processes or from your code. BAs will need to validate, prioritize, and ensure the right context is used for the test scenarios.	Analysts will need to facilitate that the right scenarios are present, and the priorities of testing them, and that the expected results are as intended.

Traditional Deliverable	AI Implications	Stepping into Leveraging AI
Business rules	AI can identify these from value steams, customer journeys, and business processes. BAs will need to simplify the rules to maximize business value and user experiences.	Analysts will need to work with business and operations teams to remove unneeded and unused rules, align rules to policies, and align them further to user performance.
User scenarios	AI can identify these from value steams, customer journeys, and business processes. BAs will need to simplify the rules to maximize business value and user experiences.	Analysts will need to work with business and operations teams to ensure that the right scenarios are identified and discussed.
Non-functional requirements	AI can identify these from common processes, service agreements, or from your code. BAs will need to simplify the rules to maximize business value and user experiences.	Analysts will need to work with business and technical teams to prioritize these and edit them to meet feasibility and strategic impacts.
Meeting agenda and notes	AI can create these, or at least a draft.	Analysts will still need to determine what info from the AI they will use, and use notes and agendas to influence others, making the notes strategic to influence action from others, vs. just straight-up notes.

Business Analysis Roles in the Future

Chapter Summary

- This chapter explores the business analyst as a knowledge worker, emphasizing the role's increasing complexity.

- It is discussed how AI is reshaping the nature of knowledge work, emphasizing the importance of adapting to these changes to stay relevant.

- The future role of the business analyst is positioned as a strategic facilitator, emphasizing the importance of aligning strategic imperatives with technology use.

Action Items

- Develop a robust learning and development plan that should include AI-related skills, strategic thinking, and a deep understanding of emerging technologies.
- Establish business analysis frameworks and methodologies that facilitate the alignment of strategic imperatives with technology.
- Facilitate open communication channels to ensure the business analyst role is actively involved in strategic planning. Start looking at how you can use the **AI Analysis Accelerator Framework** to align initiatives to strategy.

These action items aim to prepare business analysts for their future role as strategic facilitators, equipped with the knowledge and skills necessary to navigate the evolving landscape of knowledge work and effectively contribute to organizational success.

Business Analysis Roles in the Future

6　Implications of AI on Business Analysis

The implications of AI on analysis work are likely to be vast! It will demand us to have an evolving skillset to adapt to the three areas that are of importance to business analysis in an AI-immersed world: productivity; the SDLC and team collaboration changes; and the business and customer processes we support.

In this chapter we will look at each of these areas and the implications in more detail. We will look at how we can be far more productive in our work when leveraging GenAI to augment and assist us with analysis work.

We will discuss how the SDLC is changing and what that means to how we collaborate with others in the process. And we will look at aspects of how our business partners and customers will experience changes from AI, and how to navigate these changes as their partners.

Vignette

Samantha Ghent

I knew we were doing this right when we saw a change in the business analysts in our organization. What did we see? We started seeing the analysts work hand in hand with value stream owners. Before this, maybe 10% would be empowered and own their role. Now, we have far more empowered, self-enabling, and engaged business analysts; engaged in the success and connection overall of their work to the organization's success. Specifically, we now see the following:

- *Business analysts drive leaders to measurable strategies, encourage leaders not to use language like "frictionless experience" and "best of class." These are not measurable, nor do they show alignment to the organization's success. Analysts are comfortably addressing these strategic gaps with confidence, facilitating meaningful metrics. Objectively assessing the value stream, identifying the gaps and partnering with the leadership/management to address the gaps using data-based evidence.*

- *Business analysts understand their role is to facilitate these outcomes and behavior change, no matter what others tell them their role is. We have specifically trained and made it clear that this is their role and these results need to be measured.*
- *Business analysts craft the details and alignment to the results. They call out whims of what some stakeholders want with the details; it's all about measurements and alignment. No longer are analysts pressured to make developers faster and more productive at the cost of delivering actual value. AI codes most of it for us. Delivering value, and fast, is far more important; it's about teamwork now, and everyone has their role.*

This was an organizational shift more than anything. We realized that, before, we did not clearly have the business analysis role and their value proposition defined well. Previously, the role was left open to every team's determination of what success is. We let cultural norms get in the way of empowering this role. Now, we are clear that the business analyst aligns strategy— business results—user behavior changes—to the team's assets, deliverables, and activities and tasks.

Adapting to an AI-Dominated Future: The Evolving Skillset

In a world rapidly being shaped by AI, there's no denying that the very nature of business analysis is undergoing a profound transformation. Knowledge workers, such as business analysts who historically have been relied upon for their specialized skills and expertise, find themselves at a crossroads. It was first thought that AI would not have a major effect on knowledge workers, or at least a delayed effect; however, evidence is proving this not to be the case.

As AI continues to demonstrate domination in data analysis, pattern recognition, and information retrieval, the age-old question arises: What is the unique value that humans bring to the professional landscape?

We are seeing that human and AI collaboration together is where the magic lies. When the human holds the context, strategy, and judgment and can lead the AI agent through the process; we can leverage AI to get not only speed and pace, but also quality and alignment.

We do not have a crystal ball into the future; however, we can observe a clearly emerging skillset. For business analysts and other knowledge workers, the following skills are very relevant to master in an AI-dominant age:

- Learn, unlearn, and relearn: With the accelerating pace of technological change, the ability to learn, unlearn, and relearn will be paramount. Professionals will need to be continuous learners, have a learning mindset, and be ready to refresh their skillset in response to shifting technologies.

- Problem-solving: AI can process vast amounts of data quickly and recognize seemingly unrelated patterns; however, business analysts have the adaptiveness, curiosity, and experimental nature to also connect what seem to be unrelated items. Together, AI and a curious business analyst will be able to problem-solve at a higher level than either alone.

- Emotional intelligence: Building relationships, empathy with human emotions, and navigating complex interpersonal dynamics are areas where business analysts thrive. AI will struggle to emulate human EQ, and human empathy will be more sought after than ever.

- Ethics: Business analysts can make thousands of ethical reasoning decisions per day against organizational policies, whereas AI makes decisions based on data. Understanding the ethical implications of algorithms and rules is critical so that AI behaves in a manner consistent with societal values.

- AI: Business analysts will need to continuously learn about AI; however, this will be less about the technical side and more about the key inputs to produce an outcome and limitations. Working side by side with AI, analysts will concentrate on setting measurements, tracing and measuring success.

- Creativity and innovation: AI can assist with diverse thinking and generating options that individuals or groups would struggle to produce. However, business analysts will need to identify real innovation, which often springs from experiences, insights, and skills. This trait will separate us from AI.

- Cross-disciplinary knowledge: As AI excels in repetitive tasks and gets better at complex thinking tasks, a broad understanding across various specializations across the value steam can allow analysts to leverage AI to help analyze and synthesize insights in unique ways. For business analysis, this includes taking from multiple disciplines, such as practices in Six-Sigma, Agile, DevOps, design thinking, innovation, scientific research, sales, marketing, and more.

While the exact skills required in the future remain elusive, one thing is certain: Skills will continue to evolve. Business analysts must stay agile, curious, and open to change. Learning will be their only safeguard in the professional world but will also enrich it with the irreplaceable value of human insight, true empathy, and creativity.

Leveraging AI as an organizational capability will not only enhance careers, it will also keep organizations from becoming irrelevant.

There are three major implications of AI for analysis in organizations.

- •Productivity
- •Team collaboration changes
- •New business models

Let's take a look at how each of these will impact how analysis is done, how they can elevate the work of analysis that professionals do, and how they can provide more value to the organization.

Productivity

AI will help analysis professionals be more productive. It will be like having multiple analysts to delegate to. Using AI as a productivity tool, analysts will still need to carefully give directions on how to complete a task, ask how the task was done, and then check the work. This requires not only prompting skills, but the ability to prompt an AI agent with the knowledge and skills of an experienced and trained business analyst.

Some of the things that AI can help analysis professionals do include

- identifying user scenarios, user stories, and alternate path scenarios for various user processes,
- helping capture workshop decisions and action items from a workshop recording,
- helping identify elements of visual models to aid in analysis,
- analyzing datasets (random or not) to derive conclusions and patterns much more quickly and accurately,
- analyzing datasets about current process performance, user insights, and datasets that may predict future performance given certain changes,
- writing embedded system documentation,
- write test case scenarios, and
- writing impact analysis summaries.

Before leveraging GenAI, many of these tasks would take days, weeks, or even months to complete. Business analysts would plan and set up meetings, and then after many meetings to gather information, they would analyze, request data from a data team, wait for the data, rework the data, plan and document more, schedule review meetings, and the cycle goes on. With GenAI, this accelerates greatly. Analysts can cut down on the number of meetings and get to better drafts, higher-quality conversations, and better data more quickly. This all presumes they have the deep business analysis skills to leverage and harmonize with GenAI to do so.

In order to harmonize with and leverage GenAI for these tasks, analysts need good prompting skills as well as good analysis skills. AI cannot do the analysis for us, we need to probe, prompt, and guide the GenAI to find the right knowledge and context for the analysis work we are doing. It's a harmonization of deep analysis skills in combination with AI that makes the difference.

Other areas of productivity in business analysis tasks include the following.

Automated Traceability: Tools Automatically Align Analysis Work

Traceability has been a major, time-consuming task for skilled analysts in the past, and most that are skilled in this would never do analysis work again without it. It is one of those indispensable skills that can save a team so much pain and work as change analysis happens mid-project.

Much of traceability can be automated! Some tools have automated tracing for years. With AI, this increases our ability to trace in various directions for more purposes. We are seeing AI create amazing efficiencies for analyzing impacts, gap analysis, cost analysis, change analysis, testing analysis, and code impact analysis. While the traceability can be automated, the requirements hierarchy definition remains a complex task for highly skilled business analysts.

This is a good example of some deep analysis skills that will be so much easier with AI, and that will provide crazy value to organizations and teams. But these also require an advanced level of business analysis skill that most analysts, teams, and organizations do not have today.

Faster Data Insights: More Data Insights on User and Customer Behaviors

Today, it takes a lot of work and organizational maturity to use data to inform what system and process changes should be implemented to improve **business results**. Most requests from business leaders to an IT group are for reports and dashboards, looking to report on historical and real-time data. Then, leaders make decisions and build work queues based on these reports, such as "Last month's sales report" and "Current sales pipeline."

With more advanced AI, analysts need to lead business leaders into using predictive and prescriptive analytics to solve their leadership tasks and customer interactions. Using predictive analytics, "Last month's sales report" may become, "Next month's sales predictions," so that a leader can adapt the team to meet the predicted sales.

Using prescriptive analytics, a sales leader may get direction from dynamic data leverage patterns and AI as to which customers or potential customers should receive more attention, or a specific sales approach.

With AI, this becomes much easier because analysts can map strategic imperatives to key measurements, to value streams and processes, and use data and AI to notify them of system performance challenges that would improve user experiences. Analysts will also be able to model and predict what changes will make a difference. This takes skill; it will not happen automatically.

More Effective Executive-Level Conversations

With changes going from idea to implementation in a matter of hours for many leveraging AI—or much faster than before as many explore what AI can do—the amount of change will increase dramatically. This will require analysts to be at the executive table more. More high-impact conversations and decisions will be happening in shortened timeframes.

This, in turn, will require analysts to have the communication and context skills to have this level of conversation, and be able to communicate complex concepts at an executive level effectively.

New Mindsets = More Productivity

 Analysts who use AI stand to gain a high performance level if they have the right mindset. While many successful analysts have the needed mindset today, many do not. Those with a mindset of "completing documentation records," or of "doing what stakeholders ask for," will struggle to thrive in this new world.

The mindset that analysts in an AI-driven world will need:

- My role is to solve problems and take advantage of opportunities for the organization, no matter what my stakeholders ask for.

- My role is to aid businesses in change; change to process, systems, rules, policies, and people. Everything I do connects to helping the business, its people, partners, and customers perform their tasks and interactions better.

- Everything I do aligns to a strategic imperative, and I am driven to connect my work and the team's work to these strategic imperatives.

- My role in documenting is limited to the purposes of creating a shared understanding from what has already been discussed or collaborated on, or to aid myself and the team in analysis. I question the value of everything that gets documented, and I seek to find more efficient ways to accomplish the same communications goals using a higher-impact communication methods.

Faster Analysis: More Analysis and Synthesis, Less Documentation

Many business analysts today complain that there is no time for actual analysis, and that they are too busy between emails, meetings, workshops, and cranking out documentation.

Great analysts are trained and experienced in a way that it becomes painfully clear that the approach of poorly planned meetings, without the right conversations happening, result in more non-value emails and replies, more poor meetings, and a whole lot of unused documentation.

Great analysts can be upwards of 100x more productive for organizations if they understand the following:

- Understand the context (or seek to understand this first), such that they can ask good questions and guide their own work and processes, rather than doing what everyone directly asks of them. For example, if a stakeholder asks an analyst to organize some meetings to elicit requirements, an experienced analyst doesn't just go and set up a series of meetings. They understand that this may be what the stakeholder thinks is needed, and it may be needed, but upon truly assessing the context, they realize that the problem is not well understood. Without this, any series of meetings will be unproductive and not even have the right people in the room, hence wasting everyone's time.

  With analysis performed on value streams, customer journeys, and processes while leveraging AI to monitor the performance, this context becomes more absolute to anyone performing business analysis and is responsible for leading the improvement process of the value stream.

- Learn how to question the value and why of literally everything, which results in actually removing 90% of the work that others "think" the analyst should do; focusing on the 10% that matters is critical to achieving **business results**. We have seen countless examples of analysts doing far too much of what everyone else is asking them to do, yet little to no value being delivered. An experienced, skilled, certified, and trained business analyst can deliver so much more by simply having the right mindset, skills, and approach in responding to requests. With AI implementations, this dynamic will only magnify these challenges and successes.

- Use analysis techniques in different contexts and with different levels of detail. Great analysts with good training and experience can use analysis techniques with a variety of different technologies and business processes and apply analysis to any domain.

  Great analysts don't just create visual models, they assess what level of detail is needed for the context, stakeholder group, and purpose of the moment. AI can help analysts create models, but an analyst who doesn't understand visual analysis models, and who doesn't think about the context, purpose, stakeholder group, and level of detail, will still not use them correctly and will be counterproductive. A well-trained analyst, with AI, will not only use the model for the right situation, context, and purpose, but will be aided by AI to be quite efficient at creating inputs to stakeholder collaborations.

Fully Leveraging Existing Skills and Techniques

Where in the past it could be a tough decision for an analyst to spend time on a time-consuming task, with AI these tasks become a no-brainer. The analyst must have the existing skills of specific analysis and collaboration techniques to leverage AI to their advantage in productivity.

SDLC and Team Collaboration Changes

How teams work to deliver and implement solutions is changing as AI takes hold. The SDLC (software development lifecycle) is changing, and this also means how we collaborate is also changing. Practices that took time and were costly can now be done so much faster, which will allow teams to enable analysis best practices more easily. As AI-driven organizations find ways to leverage AI, the entire SDLC will change.

Tasks that used to take months will take mere seconds! The rate of change that organizations can tolerate will accelerate to levels that were previously unimaginable.

Teams will heavily focus on integrating decisions and problem-solving at a speed that will require a completely different approach and level of collaboration across the organization.

Assessing Where Your Organization is at, and Seeing the Future SDLC

To determine how dramatic these changes will be in your organization, use the following series of attribute statements.

These are numbered in order of the level of maturity your organization may currently be at, with traditional waterfall practices first, and more agile moving down. Use this to find where you have been, where you are at, and what needs to happen next.

A word of caution: If your organization currently aligns to the attributes in number 1, skipping ahead will require a strong focus on cultural and organizational change management.

1. Attributes of those in traditional/waterfall ways of working:
   - We plan initiatives a year in advance and fund them the year before, with allocated amounts for each project initiative.
   - We scope out projects in order to fund and budget them with solutions already in mind.
   - We hand off the defined high-level scope to a project manager and business analyst, and they need to get requirements done fast with +/- 10% estimates to implement so we can approve the project.

- The business analyst does requirements work with detailed specification documents that get handed off to development teams.
- Changes to requirements once handed off are painful and may be managed by a change control process for larger projects.
- The analyst is expected to be an expert in the system.

2. Attributes of those moving towards more agile ways of working:
- We define smaller increments of work to deliver.
- We work in small, generalist teams.
- We use agile tools and methods.
- We are not getting feedback from users on what we build until we fully release.

3. Attributes of those starting to become agile in how they work:
- We work from a user point of view.
- Our sprints/iterations that we work on are releasable.
- Our small teams are truly cross-functional (frontend, backend, API, and data, QA, Dev, all on one team).
- We are working much more closely with business teams and users as we build.
- We are still promising features and deadlines over more holistic metrics and feedback.

4. Attributes of those that are truly incorporating agile ways of working:
- We fund problems to solve then assign a team to work on solving them.
- We measure problems from a user point of view and focus on chasing better user success with our work.
- We dynamically prioritize and build the backlog based on end-user feedback.
- We commit to solving user problems, rather than predefined scope, and we align our solution options strategically to leverage our strategic, product, and technical roadmaps.
- We proactively get regular feedback from users on existing and new features as part of our plans and regular processes for each sprint/iteration, release, and ongoing.
- We harness user insight data to give us insights into user needs and performance of how our product meets user needs.

5. Attributes of those embarking on successful AI-driven work with insightful analysis:
- We are regularly using **hypotheses and experiments**.
- We are much more user focused; everything is from a user point of view.
- We constantly measure and monitor the impact of our frequent (daily/weekly) releases.

6. Attributes of those showing mature AI-driven development with insightful analysis enabled to maximize value delivery:
   - We have value streams defined.
   - We have customer journeys mapped out and aligned to products and services.
   - We have **assets** created and updated that are used regularly to facilitate and make decisions.
   - We have processes and data mapped to the products and services.
   - Measurements are defined and tracked for the user and automatic processes.
   - We have built dashboards showing us how the process is performing and highlighting variances.
   - With process variances, we get recommendations to optimize or fix things.
   - We can easily select to create a test environment and model the recommended changes, changing the input data and scenarios used.

We have seen these practices work over the years to measure critical value streams. We know that evaluating solution performance is an important part of business analysis—the *BABOK® Guide* Knowledge Area Solution Evaluation and Monitoring[1] has called this out as a business analyst's knowledge area for many years. Today, with AI advancements, enabling this type of analysis and alignment from strategy to the implementation details is more approachable, practical, feasible, and more valuable than ever.

We can now more easily do this continuously rather than hope we have time and budget to look back and evaluate what we have implemented. It will no longer serve us to "move onto the next requirements phase" and skip evaluating how well we implemented something. We need to change to evaluating and monitoring solutions and processes continuously and use this data to guide the next things to be done.

Influences from many disciplines, frameworks, and methodologies is the magic of business analysis. The new frontier of business analysis connects parts of the value chain, value streams, and customer journeys.

---

1. International Institute of Business Analysis (IIBA). *A Guide to the Business Analysis Body of Knowledge (BABOK® Guide)*, v. 3. 2015.

New Organizational Processes for Alignment and Prioritization

An AI-first organization will need to be clear in its architecture. Business agility is dependent on the ability to outpace competitors. Integrating AI into the value stream requires a quantum shift in how team tasks are prioritized, as well as role types, allocated resources, and value delivered. Below are our thoughts on how organizations can traverse to the age of AI:

- Reevaluate task hierarchies: Traditional task hierarchies are likely to become a thing of the past. Some tasks will become automated, some require human–AI collaboration, and some are best left to humans. This new hierarchy will drive resource allocation and project prioritization.

- Agile frameworks: Given the speed of developments in AI technology and how it is applied, organizations should embrace agile methodologies. The iterative approach of agile methods is perfect for the rapid AI-changing landscape.

- Set up AI ethics committees: Business rules must be monitored closely in the AI world. Ethics committees will need to govern AI implementations, ensuring social positivity.

- Training and upskilling: The speed of AI development will mean that the only way professionals will survive is through continuous training. The business analyst role will shift. Organizations need continuous training programs to ensure skills are developed that complement AI to perform emotional intelligence, complex asset linkage, creative thinking, and advanced problem-solving.

- Data management: Data in an AI world will become critical. Data connection to value streams will provide context to data relevance, and excellent governance and management practices will become paramount. Data security and data quality will continue to be important, especially since information value will continue to increase.

- Stakeholder collaboration: AI will increase the speed of decision-making; therefore, the integrity between **assets** will be critical. Incorrect structuring, tracing, and unclear dependencies will potentially be catastrophic. Stakeholders will need to be confident that value streams, business rules, and relevant data are true and correct.

New Business Models

 AI is enabling and suggesting new business models to every industry. This includes new business and customer processes.

Business analysis is at the forefront of the skills needed to help business teams, leaders, vendors, and technology teams define, plan, analyze, and ensure that the AI ideas and models are implemented with strategic alignment. Without business analysis, organizations risk precious time and resources chasing the wrong solutions or implementing in ways that could backfire. AI needs to make an organization's internal and external customers, users, and partners better off, while making business sense and creating results. This is not an easy equation. This takes deep business analysis skills to bring the goals, metrics, ideas, and details together.

Analysis skills are needed to help with these changes by

- assessing the AI-predicted new business models or new products,

- helping assess which AI capabilities are likely to improve a business or customer process based on strategic performance and metrics,

- defining the process metrics that the organization needs AI to improve to make the effort worth doing,

- evaluating current process performance, and where AI can improve performance,

- analyzing end-to-end customer and user experiences to determine whether AI ideas will help the process overall without negatively impacting other processes,

- defining **hypotheses and experiments** to test the new processes, and tracking the results of the process performance,

- defining the various user scenarios that need to be tracked, tested, and performance measured with potential changes, and

- communicating and helping the business units and customers accept the changes, and tracking where users are not adapting and working to update the process to meet user needs better.

New Skills and Focus for Business Analysts that will Evolve with AI

As we continue to embark on experiencing and learning about how AI can help us be more productive, make the SDLC better, and change our organizations' business models, we will constantly be challenged to learn new skills to keep up.

We all experience the new skills and knowledge that come with new technology. We are learning what GenAI is and is not, how best to use it, and more. We are playing with the new tools that come out and experimenting with the various use cases we hear about from others. This will continue and must continue.

As far as skills for business analysis goes, this means continuous learning. If you are not learning, you are not growing.

In the next few chapters, we discuss the impact on skills, how to develop them, and steps to move forward in this ever changing and ambiguous time.

Chapter Summary

- AI will bring about changes in three areas of analysis: Productivity, the SDLC and how we collaborate, and how we enable new business models.

- The implications of AI for the business analysis role may be large or gigantic depending on where your organization is at today. The changes to analysis will impact other roles as well; roles that are likely already going through their own transformation.

- Some individuals and organizations have a big leap to make to adapt their practices.

Action Items

- Take a look at the implications in this chapter. Which are you most concerned about?
- Where do you fit in the attributes along the path to more AI readiness?
- How do these implications impact the business analysis role in your organization? Other roles?

These action items aim to prepare analysts for their future role with AI. Some organizations have a larger gap than others to effectively improve competitiveness within the marketplace.

Implications of AI on Business Analysis

7 Future Skills and Competency

The skills needed to perform well in business analysis are changing. The future skills will need to be of a higher level compared to the current expected skills for many in the role.

In this chapter we will discuss how those performing business analysis will level up in the underlying competencies of critical thinking, problem-solving and analysis tasks and techniques, as well as increase their knowledge of AI and business strategy.

The need to level up also comes under the basic business analysis skills necessary in order to leverage the use of AI to augment the role.

We will also discuss how AI will impact the pace of skill development and what this means to skill development overall for those that do business analysis work.

Vignette

Remi Clarke: A business analysis manager in Samantha Ghent's organization

I am preparing for a meeting with my business analysis management team and HR. I am working with HR to train our analysis team on the old management techniques we will be letting go of, and the new ones we are adopting. We need to focus less on individual outputs, and more on the skills and organizational outcomes. We have redesigned how we track performance, which has impacted everything from our job descriptions, performance reviews, skills we track, and the criteria by which we measure performance.

This is a huge change for the organization, but critical to our AI and analysis first approach. The truth is that ALL of our teams need to understand AI and analysis at some level for us to perform.

We need the business analysis management team to really understand, embrace, and lean into a very new way of thinking. A new way of managing and leading the analysts, and analysis for the organization as a whole.

Today we are focused on

- *identifying the skills that no longer serve us,*
- *identifying the skills critical to success in analysts,*
- *identifying the analysis skills everyone in the organization needs,*
- *how analysts will facilitate these skills in others,*
- *how we will cultivate, build, and measure these skills, and*
- *how these skills tie into the new ways of working.*

Leveling Up

 As technology and AI advance, skills are changing fast, and continue to change faster for most professional roles. LinkedIn recently published a report that shows that the skills employees need for a given position have shifted by around 25% since 2015; by 2027, this number is expected to double.[1]

Business analysis is not immune to this trend. In fact, we would argue it is impacted more than this average.

As AI levels up, we will need to as well. The increased integration of AI into our everyday work, projects, products, and business operations signifies not just an operational shift, but also a skillset transformation for everyone, and business analysts are no exception. As AI is integrated into the tools used, the business processes, and the changes in the SDLC, the skills must be elevated. In this brave new world, the level of complexity and change is driving and will continue to drive elevated skills compared to what analysts have today.

Business analysis in an AI and analysis driven organization will require underlying competencies that are used in many professional roles, as well as more specific analysis technique skills. The underlying competencies are those used in many roles, disciplines, and professions. These often take time to build, require mentoring and feedback, and get more difficult to apply in complex situations.

> In an AI-driven world, the complexity and change will demand these competencies to level up in order to thrive and survive.

Teams, organizations, and individuals that focus on and uplift these skills will reap the rewards, with work getting done faster and of a higher significance and relevance.

---

1. https://economicgraph.linkedin.com/content/dam/me/economicgraph/en-us/PDF/skills-first-report-2023.pdf

Leveling Up Underlying Soft Skills Competencies

 With the emergence of more AI and the speed at which a higher volume of work can be done in organizations, more change-related skills will be needed to facilitate decisions big and small. The velocity of change and decisions will increase dramatically. This will take an elevated level of skill as these decisions impact many internal and external groups.

Communication

Communication skills, including written, verbal, and listening, are a longstanding and important underlying competency for analysts. With more AI in an AI-driven world, the complexities and rate of change will make communication skills even more important.

For example, communicating AI insights into understandable and actionable recommendations for stakeholders and groups from diverse backgrounds and levels becomes crucial. Analysts will need to refine and level up their communication skills, ensuring they can explain complex AI concepts in straightforward terms and drive alignment and decisions across teams, leaders, and partners. Senior management engagement will become more relevant as business analysis becomes more prevalent at the strategic decision-making level.

Communicating the chain of value from **business results** to **user behavior changes** to **hypotheses** and down to the work of the **deliverables** and **team tasks and activities** is a key business analysis skill. Using **assets** as a tool to help communicate is also an important aspect of success.

The techniques analysts use for building and showing this competency include the following:

- Visual thinking and modeling: Thinking and creating visual models to communicate complex information, and then connecting details to one another in ways that show how details are connected to the context overall.

- Conceptual thinking and modeling: Thinking about how detailed information relates to the larger picture and finding ways to communicate these concepts to stakeholders.

- Visualization tools: Using tools to graphically represent data and AI insights.

- Storytelling: Crafting narratives around data and scenarios to drive shared understanding.

- Questioning skills used in stakeholder conversations.

- Structured text: Decomposition and abstraction of complex concepts in structured text.

Behavioral Characteristics

The rapidly changing environment we are in, and which will continue, demands resilience, adaptability, and a growth mindset. As AI tools redefine roles, analysts need to demonstrate their willingness to evolve and their drive to navigate new challenges through the following:

- Emotional intelligence: Recognizing our own emotions and how they impact others. Recognizing others' emotions and adapting our behavior accordingly. Both are crucial for maximizing team dynamics in an evolving workspace.

- Self-assessment: Regularly reflecting on skills, experience, feedback, personal strengths, and areas for growth.

- Growth mindset: Embracing challenges, persisting in the face of setbacks, and understanding that effort drives growth.

- Organization and time management.

- Adaptability.

Ethical Decision-Making

Ethics is a longstanding underlying competency of business analysis, and with AI, it's more necessary than ever. Given concerns around AI ethics, such as bias and data privacy issues, analysts will need to enhance skills around ethical decision-making, and consider even more where AI may be making decisions, as well as evaluating whether these decisions are at risk of not aligning ethically to the organizational values, regulations, and societal ethics.

The techniques analysts use for building and showing this competency include the following:

- Ethics and values checklist: Assessing user scenarios and data against defined enterprise values and ethics policies.

- Bias audits: Creating and using checklists to detect and mitigate AI-generated bias.

- Privacy impact assessments: Evaluating how AI may impact data and user privacy, and running scenario-driven automated tests.

- Ethics committees: Analysts can facilitate ethics committees to help ensure that policies and business rules are implemented correctly.

Change Management

In the past, analysts with change management skills have been real gems. Those that have been able to assess and communicate the changes to each user group, and create comfort in the change with those groups, are often high-performing business analysts. With the rapid technological advancements we are seeing with AI, resistance to change can and will be a potentially significant impediment. Change management competencies will be increasingly needed to help teams and departments navigate and adapt to the transformations, workflow changes, and fears brought about with increased AI use.

The techniques analysts use for building and showing this competency include the following:

- ADKAR change model[1]: A structured approach that looks at awareness, desire, knowledge, ability, and reinforcement.

- Stakeholder analysis: Understanding and addressing the needs and concerns of those affected by change.

- Communication plans: Structured strategies and communications for informing stakeholders about changes they will experience and need to change in themselves.

- Value streams: Useful for understanding interested stakeholders, managing or receiving the workflow.

Continuous Learning

Change is constant and so are the skills and techniques analysts use to get work done. So much of the business analysis mindset and techniques are changing. We will need to learn new techniques, new tools to use existing techniques, new nuances to our current techniques, and new knowledge sets to be able to navigate an AI world with powerful business analysis. The dynamic nature of AI means analysts can't afford to be complacent. A commitment to continuous learning, whether through conferences, industry events, courses, workshops, and self-study, will be essential to stay up to date on both AI, business analysis, and evolving business landscapes.

1. ww.prosci.com/methodology/adkar

The techniques analysts use for building and showing this competency include the following:

- Observation: Seeing others perform a task that you need to learn.

- Mentoring: Having a more experienced colleague to provide feedback, ask questions of, and to guide progress.

- Online courses: Utilizing the ever growing AI and business analysis courses available online.

- Workshops and conferences: Participating in skills and industry workshops and conferences.

- Peer review: Engaging in discussions with other analysts to share work examples and gain knowledge.

- Lessons learned: Retrospective evaluation of opportunity for improvement.

Collaboration and Teamwork

If the word "silo" resonates with your organization, AI is one thing that just might break the paradigm and move the needle to break the silos down. As AI further integrates into business operations, technology, and everything we do, cross-functional collaboration becomes a critical piece to deliver meaningful change and updates.

Business analysts can improve and increase collaboration effectiveness by leveraging the connection between **business results**, **user behavior changes**, **hypotheses**, **assets**, and how these drive the connection to the **deliverables** and **team tasks and activities**.

Analysts will need to work closely with data scientists, IT teams, vendors, leaders, and business units, necessitating strong teamwork and collaboration skills. This involves

- facilitating diverse stakeholder groups through decision-making, experiments, summaries of datasets and results, and process simulations, and

- collaborating with various roles and levels to bring about creative thinking, critical thinking, innovation, and decision-making at a sustainable pace while moving the organization forward.

AI integration often spans various business units and departments. Analysts must elegantly navigate these cross-departmental collaborations, fostering a sense of shared understanding and purpose and garnering strategic alignment.

This includes building skills in the following:

- Stakeholder management: Understanding and managing expectations, concerns, and needs of different stakeholders.

- Facilitation: Leading collaborative stakeholder and team sessions, workshops, or brainstorming meetings effectively.

- Negotiation: Balancing various stakeholders' needs to create decisions that all can support and align strategically.

The techniques analysts use for building and showing this competency include the following:

- Cross-functional workshops: Engaging diverse teams in joint problem-solving sessions.

- Online collaboration: Using online tools to brainstorm as a group virtually, and vote, comment, and work a collaborative process online together with high engagement.

- Conflict resolution: Using techniques to identify, address, and resolve disagreements, conflicting ideas, and priorities among stakeholder groups and teams.

- Metrics: Helping people focus on the value and purpose. Once a common goal is shared, collaboration is enhanced.

Human-Centric Design Thinking

Looking at AI as a "technical" or "data" thing will not work. The business analysis role is the front and center role to bring the human element to the work. Amidst all of the process, data, rules, and algorithms, the end users' needs and experiences should remain central, and the analysts' role is to make this happen! Skills in human-centric design thinking will ensure that AI-driven solutions make the user experience even better. This is not about just an isolated screen or interaction, but looking at the customer journey more holistically, measuring it, and connecting the results to the strategic intent of the organization.

We use **user behavior changes** aligned to **business results** to keep stakeholders and the team focused with a human-centered thinking process. **Assets** also play a huge part in this as we create many of them from a customer point of view.

The techniques analysts use for building and showing this competency include the following:

- Empathy mapping: Collaboratively understanding the users' feelings, needs, and challenges in the current and future desired state.

- Rapid prototyping: Using low or no code solutions to develop rapid prototypes.

- Customer journey mapping: Mapping out the users' experiences, emotions, and interactions with a product, system, or service.

- Mind mapping: Exploring relationships of key concepts to present a clear view of complex problems.

The role of the analyst is not diminished but rather elevated if we embrace the upskilling needed to make business analysts hugely impactful. While AI can provide the tools and the data, it is the refined and upgraded skills of the analyst and analysis pieces of the organization that will transform the work into tangible business outcomes. Analysts with these enhanced skills will be poised not only to thrive but to lead in this new AI world.

In an AI-driven organization, change is a constant. These foundational competencies will enable analysts to remain nimble, adaptable, relevant, and effective at facilitating value among teams with technological possibilities and strategic business outcomes.

Leveling Up Underlying Critical-Thinking and Problem-Solving Competencies

Critical-Thinking Skills

Critical thinking is so important in every aspect of using AI. Whether you are using AI to bring more productivity to your tasks, using it as part of a team in an SDLC, or using it to run a business process, critical thinking is of paramount importance.

GenAI and data analytics are significant parts of leveraging AI in all aspects of our work. Both also require an understanding of critical thinking and a strong application of it to implement and get good results.

We will need to leverage our critical-thinking skills when using GenAI to assist us in creating our assets we use for analysis, everything from visual models, user scenarios, testing scenarios, data analysis, and more. We will also need critical thinking to define our hypotheses and experiments, and user behavior changes.

Critical thinking is paramount when using AI for several reasons in business analysis work. Many have concerns about AI "telling the truth," and what we are finding is that when AI is used in the right context, and with the right prompting skills, this is dramatically reduced.

For example:

- Differentiating fact from fiction: With GenAI, we can generate text and/or other outputs that sound realistic but may be inaccurate. Without good prompting (which requires understanding what you are asking for), and critical thinking, users may accept the AI's output as truth. Prompting without analysis skills, or with the wrong context, can lead to misinformation and misunderstanding. It is easy for an unskilled business analyst to use AI and result in poorly performing on everything from work collaboration processes, configuration decisions, testing, decision-making, and recommendations, to software systems and products with poor user processes, interactions, and logic.

   With data analytics, it can also be easy to take AI-driven data analysis as fact, when the data used may not be the correct source data, may not be complete data, may have low-quality data, or we may be blind to what the denominator of the data population being used is. All of this without a critical-thinking lens can cause analysts, teams, and leaders to make poor decisions and/or implement processes that will not yield the desired results.

   AI can do amazing data analysis on unstructured data as well; however, understanding data analysis is key to understanding the range of interpretations of the answers AI provides. For example, when we asked an AI tool to analyze 22,000 rows of unstructured data, it did truly amazing analysis, with sourced code to see how it performed the analysis. But, without the skills to critically think about what denominator is being used with the analysis performed, the ability to read the source code when we asked the AI how it got to the answers, and the ability to ask further questions to clarify the data and answers, the facts could easily be misinterpreted (seen as hallucinating or lying from some perspectives). The skills to ask the right questions to the AI agent about how they have gotten to the answers is key! This requires deep skills in the task we are asking AI to help with.

- Ethical implications: AI can generate content that is biased, inappropriate, or even offensive. Users need to critically assess the prompts, data source, data quality, and outputs to ensure the content aligns with ethical guidelines, policies, law, and the values that the organization upholds.

- Data reliability: AI models use a lot of data, and this may contain massive quality issues, bias, and/or just plain false information. Critical thinking is required to question and validate the source, quality, and accuracy of this information. Business analysis work is at the heart of this with skills to analyze processes, data flow, workflows, and data quality. Critical thinking is a needed skill in addition to the specific analysis technique skills to bring together the best understanding of how reliable the data actually is, as well as helping make decisions on how reliable the data needs to be in order to meet the intended **business results**.

- Over-reliance on AI: As AI tools become more sophisticated, and sometimes even invisible to users using various software products, there is a risk that we might rely on them too heavily, forgetting our critical thinking and judgment. Critical thinking ensures that humans remain in the decision-making loop, using AI as a tool rather than a crutch.

- Interpreting ambiguities: AI-generated content can be ambiguous. Critical thinking helps in discerning the output, and the intended need for a given context. Context is king, and business analysis is the critical piece to ensure that context of the business, organization, industry, users, and technical ecosystem are taken into account on how we use and leverage AI within our processes, systems, products, and customer interactions.

- Security concerns: GenAI models not only have defined data sources, but they can also ingest data back in and dynamically include this in the model and its learning. Users need to critically evaluate the content, the source of the content, and evaluate when and if it is appropriate to also share data back with the model and/or sources. Critical thinking helps in evaluating the sources in relationship to the context, and to ensure that data is evaluated and scrubbed appropriately before providing data to an AI model.

- Understanding context: AI models do not truly "understand" context in the way humans do, and business analysis success is all about context. We need to think critically about whether the AI's response is appropriate for the specific situation and need that we have, or if it's simply a regurgitation of learned patterns. This also carries into the prompts we use (visible or embedded prompts) that also provide context to an AI model. Asking an AI about insurance policy norms and personal auto insurance policy norms in the state of Texas would provide very different answers. Critical thinking in how we prompt and ask for information is really important to using it successfully.

- Decision-making: In scenarios where AI provides suggestions that influence decisions, such as medical diagnoses, customer service responses, or financial advice, critical thinking is vital to ensure the outcomes are based on sound reasoning and not just possibilities. We can use business analysis to experiment with datasets for scenarios and generate a quality run showing how a specific confirmation would run against a set of real data in the context of the organization and process being updated using AI.

- System thinking: Understanding how various elements within systems relate and interact is especially crucial when integrating AI tools within existing business processes, user workflows, and for evaluating ethics.

- Hypothesis thinking: Formulating **hypotheses** and designing **experiments** to learn more.

The above list shows how there are a lot of critical-thinking aspects. That is how important the critical-thinking skills are! Critical thinking is a safeguard that ensures our analysis—when used with AI—is used responsibly and effectively. Enhanced critical-thinking skills will accelerate the team's work and produce higher-quality results overall.

Complex Problem-Solving Skills

In an AI-driven world, the complexity and scope of problems, solutions, and the work we do multiplies. While AI tools can provide productivity, human analytical thinking is needed to contextualize these findings, ask the right questions, and discern subtle patterns and implications, given each unique context and strategy.

AI systems will take over more and more routine analytical tasks. Business analysts will increasingly need to work on more complex, ambiguous challenges that require innovative solutions. This necessitates elevated problem-solving skills, integrating both logical reasoning and creative thinking.

Problem-solving in complex and innovative domains, like AI and other context we are in, is what drives the need for continuous analysis using **assets**, and **hypotheses**-driven work. This, aligned to the **user behavior changes** and the **business results** is what helps us make sure we are working on the right **deliverables** and **team tasks and activities**. Without this structured thinking that business analysis facilitates, it is simply too easy to waste time working on the wrong things.

Techniques that analysts use for building and showing this competency include the following:

- Root cause analysis: Identifying the underlying cause of problems.

- Brainstorming sessions: Encouraging creative thinking to address challenges.

- Decision matrix: Defining the criteria and ranking and evaluating potential solutions options and alternatives based on the predefined criteria.

- Assumption analysis: Assumptions are identified, tracked, and managed.

Level-Up Knowledge of AI and Business Acumen

AI Literacy

It is not likely to be business analysts who are developing AI models themselves, but they should have a foundational understanding of AI, machine learning, and their capabilities. This means understanding how models are trained, how they find patterns to develop their capabilities, how they dynamically update, and how they can create potential biases.

A technique analysts use for building and showing this competency is prompt engineering. This involves techniques for prompting AI to get different results and asking questions in different ways to maximize the **business results** needed for the process and **user behavior change**.

> Prompt engineering is a lot like the "structured conversation" and "requirements decomposition" skills analysts are typically taught. This is a common thinking style for analysts, and it should be! It is about providing context, critical thinking, asking good questions, questioning what you get back, and curiously digging within a context to move forward using the following:
>
> - Data and context analysis: Techniques to identify and correct biases in training and source data.
> - **Hypotheses and experiments**: Defining and running these to test assumptions about the LLM the AI is using.
> - Critical thinking: Thinking about and asking AI-driven chatbots how they got to their answers, having a conversation with a GenAI tool that critically thinks about the provided answers, or the configuration of the API driving the conversation and output from AI.

Deepened Domain Expertise and Business Acumen

AI can process vast amounts of data. Interpreting it in a meaningful business context requires deep domain expertise or strong critical-thinking skills to be able to question and validate the results within the context of the work being done.

This becomes important as we use continuous analysis and **assets** to facilitate the right conversation with business leaders and stakeholders about the expected **business results** and expected **user behavior changes.** We use the **assets** to ensure that the scenarios we test for and analyze align to these higher-level **business results** and **user behavior changes**.

Analysts will need to understand their industry and organizational drivers, complexities, intricacies, trends, and challenges more than ever, acting as a facilitator of AI output and actionable insights.

This is different from being a system SME that many analysts find themselves in the role of today. This is domain expertise at a higher level, and it is about being able to connect and think critically about how the details drive the bigger picture.

Techniques analysts use for building and showing this competency include the following:

- Value stream mapping: Defining, looking at, and analyzing how value is created and delivered for our end users (internally) and how this interfaces with customers and suppliers (externally), looking for opportunities to improve the time effectiveness for users, the quality of the inputs they need, and the outputs they produce.

- Customer journey mapping: External facing, defining, and looking holistically at the context and journey a customer takes to get something done. This looks outside system boundaries and at emotions of users and context before and after they use a product or system.

- Industry research: Keeping up on regularly reviewing industry reports, publications, and case studies, blogs, articles, and more.

- Benchmarking: Understanding and comparing process performance from others to our own.

- SWOT analysis: Looking at strengths, weaknesses, opportunities, and threats related to the market and industry we are in.

- Metrics: Measuring user behavior changes such as purchasing, repurchasing, and referring.

Deepened Business Strategy Knowledge

 More than ever, business analysts are going to need to be linked to strategy and strategic intent. Analysts will play a pivotal role in shaping the long-term strategy of organizations, and more immediately they will play a central role in connecting strategy to the work teams are doing with AI. This requires a forward-thinking mindset, understanding the industry you are in, understanding current trends, and uniquely leveraging AI to deliver on strategy.

Connecting the organization's strategic intent to business results, user behavior changes, hypotheses, and the details of what is delivered in the deliverables and team tasks and activities is a business analysis imperative!

Great business analysis means "thinking" for the business when they are too busy, distracted to do so, procrastinating, or simply don't know how to start. This is not about what they asked us to do, or the solution they think needs to be implemented. It's about connecting business value to their idea so that the team can actually align the work to deliver value.

Analysts who do this today get promoted!

An example of this would be appropriately challenging and partnering to get a better result. In order to succeed, many analysts will need to get comfortable being uncomfortable. This means that when stakeholders ask for something, you are comfortable with the discomfort of challenging the ask, and following a structured conversation and process to elicit information that will help everyone align better. It's a play for long-term success and comfort over short-term pacifying comfort in the moment.

The techniques analysts use for building and showing this competency include the following:

- Scenario planning: Imagining and defining various future scenarios based on current trends and future predicted trends.

- PESTLE analysis: Evaluating **p**olitical, **e**conomic, **s**ocial, **t**echnological, **l**egal, and **e**nvironmental factors that could influence our context, business, system, product.

- Business Model Canvas[1]: Describes how a business creates and delivers value to customers.

- Blue Ocean Strategy[2]: The simultaneous pursuit of differentiation and low cost to open up a new market space and create new demand. It is about creating and capturing uncontested market space, thereby making the competition irrelevant.

Leveling Up the Foundations of Business Analysis

Not only do these underlying competencies and knowledge need to level up, but the very basics of business analysis does as well. Most who perform business analysis have never been formally trained or mentored in the most common analysis techniques.

Visual modeling techniques, such as state transition diagrams, decision tables, data flow diagrams, and many more, are the foundations to analyze users' workflow, data, rules, and process. These are the foundations of getting users and technology aligned. AI does not change the concept that this analysis is still needed. In fact, it will make it clearer that these skills are needed because those who do perform this analysis with augmented AI will outperform those who do not.

1. See, for example, Osterwalder, A.,and Pigneur,Y.Business Model Generation: A Handbook for Visionaries, Game Changers, and Challengers. Wiley. 2010.

2. Chan Kim, W., and Mauborgne, R.A. Blue Ocean Strategy. Harvard Business Review Press. 2015.

A business analyst who does not understand state transition diagrams, for example, will not be able to ask AI to create one, nor evaluate the quality of what is created, nor understand the need to review such logic with the stakeholders in order to validate test automations. They will also not understand and be able to analyze the opportunity to simplify the number of state transitions, to simplify the user experience, and align this experience to strategic goals. State transition diagrams are an example of a business analysis visual modeling technique and of analysis that helps drive the various states of an object in a process.

Yes, we know, we are getting nerdy and technical here. Let's imagine our same medical appointment process from previous chapters; a medical appointment as many "states." It can be scheduled, confirmed, cancelled, rescheduled, and even perhaps other states like pending approval, or no show, for example. These states all have triggers, and actions that transition them from one to any other. These need to be understood, analyzed for the user experience, aligned to the strategic intent, simplified as much as possible to meet the strategic intent, and tested. AI can help, but only a trained business analyst knows how to recognize when a process has "states," and what technique to use to analyze them, and the skills to do so.

"States" are just one of many business analysis concepts that have been around for a long time. It will continue to be an important part of the role and ensuring the right changes are delivered.

The Speed of Skill Development in an AI-Driven World

We have all experienced the unprecedented change happening as technology and AI drive business change. This has a direct and immediate impact on the pace at which business analysts must develop and refine their skills. We must intensify our skill development!

Let's look further at some of the dynamics of this accelerated learning curve.

Technological Evolution

Technology has an exponential curve, and AI is proving no different. Analysts need to continually update their understanding and techniques because they will keep evolving like other technologies have. AI will likely accelerate faster than previous technologies and be on a faster exponential curve. Change is the only constant! Business analysis, in some ways, uses many of the same skills, techniques, and competencies and will continue to see huge amounts of change in how we use these skills and the context in which we need to apply them. This is no small effort. Analysts will need to continuously learn and assimilate new knowledge and skills in how to apply the tried-and-true business analysis skills and mindset in quickly changing contexts.

Dynamic Business Ecosystem

Business is changing fast too, and our business partners will be constantly learning new things. Their ideas on what will move their business forward will change as they constantly see, experience, and learn new things! Nothing is linear or predictable as it may have been in the past. AI has enabled capabilities that demand a more fluid and adaptable approach. Skills that were relevant a year ago might need fine-tuning for a new context, or even overhauling today, and again tomorrow!

The Need for Immediate Application

Learning in today's world is different. We can no longer take weeks to learn a skill. It's about small chunks, fast learning, and applying knowledge immediately. Knowledge acquisition is the first, and fast piece, then the immediate application is where the real learning comes. Analysts must swiftly translate their newly acquired knowledge into action, then practice, get feedback, reflect, and learn more, practice more, and continuously learn. This "learn-and-apply" cycle needs to be rapid, and with feedback loops incorporated into the mix, this will keep learning relevant.

Interdisciplinary Integration

The fusion of AI into various business functions and cross-functional customer journeys and value streams means that analysts cannot operate in silos. They must quickly grasp concepts from diverse business units and user groups. They need space to think, reflect, and integrate their knowledge with their mission, taking time to critically think and connect the pieces that they are the only ones seeing, then determine what action to take based on connecting the seemingly disparate, yet very connected, concepts in creating **business results** for their organization.

Continuous Learning Imperative

Lifelong, daily learning is the new norm. Learning to learn and constantly looking for what is the most important thing to learn next is a mindset business analysts will need now more than ever. They will find themselves in perpetual learning mode, continually seeking out courses, workshops, articles, readings, and peer interactions to stay up to date. Topics will be related to business analysis, their industry, technology in general, and self-improvement, among others.

A "learning debt" is what will develop if continuous learning and adapting does not happen. This is when we are not keeping up with learning new skills, new mindsets, and new approaches to our work. Many organizations have massive learning debt, and this needs to be addressed to thrive now and in the future.

Cultural and Global Changes

AI is being leveraged all over the globe and in all industries, which means AI tools are not just for business or technology. AI has societal, cultural, and geopolitical implications. Keeping up to date on these areas will help analysts build trust with business and technology leaders in their organization. They will work together to determine the intricacies of selecting options to implement strategic intent, and then decide on the details of how to leverage or prompt AI compared to how others do, and which user groups are impacted. Analysts must remain attuned to these broader shifts with the relationship to the details, adjusting their skills and strategies as they work.

Strategies to Keep Up

At such a breakneck pace, how can business analysts ensure they are contributing and adding value as their leaders expect? Here are some examples of how:

- Continuous learning/training: Organizations must prioritize and invest in continuous training programs, ensuring that analysts have access to the latest tools, techniques, mindset hacks, methodologies, and best practices.

- Networking and collaboration: Engaging with industry peers, joining professional associations, and attending conferences can provide insights into emerging trends and best practices.

- Mentorship: Establishing mentor–mentee relationships can offer guidance, self- awareness, provide perspective, expertise, and accelerate skill development.

- Feedback mechanisms: Constructive feedback, from peers, leaders, and stakeholders, can help identify areas of focus.

With the whirlwind pace of AI, and the changes to our organizations, staying static is synonymous with being left behind, and with becoming obsolete. The accelerated rate of skill development for business analysts is a necessity and an imperative for organizations. Business analysis must happen, no matter if it is the analyst's role or another role or title. Organizations must develop these skills to keep up and ensure that the strategic alignment is happening all the way through to the detailed implementation and monitoring of AI.

By embracing the skills challenge head-on, analysts can position themselves at the forefront of business innovation, leadership, strategic enablement within the organization, and guiding organizations toward a prosperous, AI-augmented future.

Chapter Summary

- Many foundational business analysis skills from the past are still needed, but they will be used in a different way.
- Influence, communication, collaboration, and other underlying leadership skills will need to be amplified in this AI-driven future, and this includes amplifying the leaders' leadership skills as well as individual contributors.
- Continuous learning and keeping up will be a challenge. We need to find ways to make this part of our routines and not let our business and deadlines get in the way. Learning debt will slow you down.

Action Items

- Take inventory of your skills (or your team/organization's).
- Build a plan to incorporate new and continuous learning into routines.

These action items aim to prepare a baseline assessment of business analysis skills. Continuous learning will be the key to successfully navigating to the skills required for futureproofinng.

8   Setting Up Business Analysts for Success

In this chapter we discuss some of the ways you can help set up yourself, team, or organization for success in business analysis.

We look at some of the challenges we see today for business analysts in getting set up for success in an AI-immersed world. And we will look at an updated view of business analysis so that it can support organizations to adapt and thrive.

Vignette

Samantha Ghent

I am in our new virtual collaboration space, waiting for Nikhil, a business analyst on the team, who will brief me on the latest update for our new product we launched last month. I am in an expansive virtual room with transparent walls that display real-time data visualizations created by AI, set up by Nikhil. A few other IT and business leaders are with us, and we discuss the product data visualizations, swipe a few panels to adjust the views, and ask a few questions to the AI agent.

Nikhil enters while we are all chatting and complements the new virtual room capabilities. "Very impressive, Ms. Ghent!"

We dive into the real matter at hand, how the new product is performing, and what is next.

The AI agent—a floating blob of light—projects a visualization of key data onto the transparent screen in the middle of the room, and the visual auto-adjusts as we discuss, ask questions, and highlight areas to chat about more.

The AI agent informs us that, based on current market data, internal data, and performance of the users, process, and systems, we have a 75% probability of meeting our goals and sales targets. Nikhil has worked with the AI agent to set up these metrics based on our previous conversations about user metrics, market strategy, and our goals.

Nikhil and the AI agent also highlight some user feedback and data insights that suggest some user experience improvements are needed. Together, we discuss the hypothesis we have of the recommended updates the AI agent is suggesting, and what we think will best create the desired result. Nikhil keeps us grounded and helps keep us focused on the goals, metrics, and various internal and external factors. Nikhil asks the AI agent to run some projections on the various options with a few tweaks we discuss. Together, we can evaluate what the possible solutions the AI has proposed would look like.

Nikhil takes some to-dos to run some manual checks on the preferred solution that the group decides to move forward with. Nikhil also analyzes and checks out the testing scenarios the AI agent develops and the changes in the AI-created visual models (process, state diagrams, sequence diagrams, decision tables, UI flows, etc.). Nikhil looks at the changes in the models the AI agent has proposed for the new solution, interprets the model changes and their impact to the user scenarios, then brings a few questions back to the business leads to ensure the scenarios are aligned to the discussion in the meeting.

In the next meeting with this same group, we ask Nikhil and the AI agent to give us more details on the proposed path, what the goals, metrics, and ROI ranges might look like, and what assumptions have gone into them.

We find a scenario we are concerned about based on Nikhil's analysis. It is one that Nikhil takes a to-do to run another experiment for analysis with the business team and validate data insights. Soon after, we are able to mitigate that scenario risk, prove the changes, run the automated tests, and deploy the changes.

Nikhil has also prepared, with the help of the AI agent, the updates dashboard to monitor our changes and the impact of them, so we can see if this is working as intended in real time, starting immediately.

Setting the Path to Success

In the future scenario described in the vignette above, the boundaries between IT, business analysis, and development blur. Collaborations become seamless, data driven, and remarkably efficient, transforming the way decisions are made and executed.

Many organizations and teams have some big barriers and challenges to making this a reality. Let's look further at what some of these challenges are.

Why Business Analysts Today are not Set Up for Success

Much of the approach to business analysis described above is actually quite intuitive, with the right mindset. In many organizations, however, business analysts have not traditionally been seen as leaders and have struggled with empowerment. This, and the challenges that come with it, happen for many reasons, such as the following:

- The business analyst role is not understood: Analysts are often seen as note-takers, system domain experts, or tactical help for project managers. This is a very misguided use of a business analyst. Many analysts have a wide span of organizational knowledge and relationships, along with many years of experience. This, coupled with the right training, can easily position them for success at a strategic level. The analyst's role is about helping organizations change through new or updated products, systems, processes, and data, and is a set of activities and skills used at high levels as well as detailed levels, connecting strategy to execution. Being perceived in the organization as a lower-level role will limit their span of realized influence.

- Where business analysts are in the organizational structure: Business analysts are often inserted as analysts in IT, assigned to an application. Though the intention may be to have them analyze the business and users and align to strategy, they are often isolated and siloed into a narrow IT scope, and narrow scope of a single application. This hurts their ability to see the impact and strategic linkage across the organization. It is often very difficult for them to assert themselves to have a larger view without risking their perception of "getting it done." They are often under heavy deadline pressure to "get requirements done so that development can start." Looking outside of their application domain can be seen as "slowing things down." With AI, this changes as development may no longer be the critical path.

- Training and skills: Most analysts have never had formal training and are prized for their system or domain knowledge. This is downright scary! The expectations of their role as a problem-solver, facilitator of decision-making, and innovator are not aligned with the training they often get. Organizations need to invest in business analysis skills and leadership development of these roles to maximize the role in an AI-driven organization.

- Communication challenges: In order to truly fulfill their role, business analysts need to communicate complex concepts and detailed information in a way that works for various audiences (technical and nontechnical, leadership, and all levels of the organization). This requires skill and support, not a cookie-cutter template. Without the right communication, the right people are not engaged in the right decisions at the right level of detail, at the right time. This is a huge challenge for organizations, and one that will only amplify with AI as a constant in organizations.

- The role is changing and evolving: Many influences over the years have impacted the role and skills analysts need to thrive. As complexity in technology and business increases, the skills of the analyst need to increase to model, analyze, and communicate through these changes as they lead groups through decisions about everything from the priorities to the details of the implementation.

Key Considerations for Success

Organizations, leaders, and analysts need to consider the following to help strengthen their role and strive to maximize their impact on positive **business results**:

- Strategic involvement: In order for business analysts to connect the details to the strategy, which is incredibly important—and will be even more so in an AI-based future— analysts need to be more involved in the context and understanding of the organizational strategy. Analysts have a unique view of the business operations and technology, unlike any other role in the organization. Invite them to facilitate strategic planning sessions and allow them to contribute insights with other leaders. Strategic planning is done through business analysis, so involve the highest competent talent in this activity. Let them hear and participate in the context. Their perspective is so unique, and with the right mindset and skills, organizations stand to gain so much from involving analysts in this critical process.

- Leadership development: Business analysts are often in situations to lead and influence. Some can step up to the opportunity, and many need some training, mentoring, and empowerment, and are so close to being huge leadership contributors. These professionals have survived and many have thrived as a bridge between business operations, customers, and technology. They have built relationships at all levels and communicated to them all. They are poised to step into higher levels of leadership and influence; they often just need a mentor, an advocate, confidence, and some training to push them into this sphere of influence.

- Networking, relationships, and visibility: Giving analysts the opportunity to present, facilitate, and speak up to share their insights from their vast customer, operations, and technical knowledge will help raise their profile, and give them more credibility throughout the organization. They may need a little mentoring at first to set the example and stage for others, but it will be worth it. Once there is an example set, the role is on the way to being "seen" by others and valued throughout the organization.

Setting Up Business Analysts for Success

- Organizational awareness: Tell the stories of how business analysts are making a difference in your organization. Educate the organization about their role and strategic importance, and how they are connecting the strategic intent to the prioritization process, to the implementation details of business process changes, operational effectiveness changes, and systems, which make users and customers more successful and align back to strategy.

By proactively promoting the value of business analysis and uplifting the leadership skills and opportunities for the analysts, the organization will better navigate the complexities and pace of an AI-driven business environment.

On a more tactical level, setting up business analysts for success involves a combination of creating the right environment, offering and actively participating in nurturing the necessary training, tools, and resources. Also, nurturing a growth mindset by demonstrating it and rewarding it will be a key component.

Tactical Steps to Foster Success

Here are some tactical steps that foster this success.

Provide Structured Onboarding

Start with a robust onboarding process, one that is more strategic than you may have today. This should not just cover the basics of the role, templates, and process. It should also robustly cover the organization's strategic vision, how it measures strategy, where it is investing in its AI and digital initiatives, and how the business analyst's role aligns with these. An onboarding process should also help them understand existing **assets**, such as value streams and customer journeys, build relationships with key stakeholders throughout the organization, and with key analysts who have actively discussed what success looks like, key challenges, and the resources to overcome them.

Many analysts come into the role inheriting a misguided idea of what it is from the organization's historical perception of a business analyst, or from a previous role at an organization that did not have a robust and modern business analyst role. It's important to set up, demonstrate, and communicate what is expected from the role, the known challenges, and resources to help.

Implementing escalation processes for analysts who feel they are not able to effectively step into the role can help. Ask questions such as the following:

- Who can the analyst go to with challenges of other roles expecting things from them that are not the vision (and what the onboarding process) called out their role and expectations to be?

- What support is in place for analysts to share with one another how they are using good analysis practices?

- What good practices have successfully worked in the organization, and what teams and analysts are able to mentor them on these practices?

- What practices is the organization looking for to elevate and encourage experimentation and failure in order to learn and grow?

- What external resources are available to analysts to continue to grow, share, and learn from external analysts and experts, and bring potential new practices into the organization?

Facilitate Access to Tools and Technology

Business analysts need good tools to do their work well, yet this cannot be the focus of the role. Equipping analysts with cutting-edge tools tailored for visual modeling, data analytics, visualization, collaboration tools, and tools to store and track **assets** (business architecture and requirements management tools) will go a long way. These tools have historically been a blessing and a curse for organizations. Those that thoughtfully use them with the right focus on the practice, not just the tool itself, have much more success. Focus on the why behind the tool and the success stories of using them. Make sure to have a "tool owner" to drive a sound strategy for how these tools will support the practices, especially if they are storing **assets** to be used as inputs to continued analysis. Just training on a tool itself does not work. AI will assist in making business analysis tools more automated.

An analogy for this is buying running shoes and wearing them to play tennis. Running shoes are built to support forward movement patterns, and tennis court shoes are more for lateral movement. The shoes are a tool but using them in a way they are not made for causes them to not work effectively and increases risk of injury, cost, and pain. The same can be said for some tools that analysts find themselves using. If not properly set up for success with the purpose, the practice, and the tool itself, the tools can cause more rework and issues than benefits.

Tools are often worth it, and well worth it. Just a word of caution on thinking a tool will be a silver bullet: The practices, and the skills to perform the practices, are a necessity in order to make the tools serve their intended purpose.

Ignite Continuous Learning Opportunities

Business analysis is a learning profession, and it requires constant learning. As stated earlier, top-performing analysts are constantly learning new business models, trends, knowledge, technology trends and skills, and, above all, they are learning analysis techniques. We must encourage and invest in continuous learning for analysts to grow their skills in analysis, facilitation, leadership, communication, and more.

Continuous learning is difficult to implement. Especially when analysts are rarely able to leave work without a mounting list of work to do. How do you fit in learning when projects are "urgent" and everyone needs everything done yesterday? Not to mention time to think and analyze!

It's not just about offering or providing training. Things like subscriptions to online learning platforms, online or live courses, workshops, and conferences are all great learning opportunities. It's about supporting and demonstrating that this time is important and valued, and then creating a culture of prioritizing the learning and practicing new skills. More on this in the next chapter.

Create and Foster a Collaborative Environment

Business analysis is a collaborative process. While analysts need solo time to think, the inputs and iterative nature of the analysis and work requires an immense amount of collaboration. It still amazes us when we hear some analysts say they are not allowed to talk to users or customers. Or that the project doesn't have time for this. Or worse, they are expected to simply write the spec document to hand off to the development team. If any of these are true of your environment, there is a big transformation that must happen.

Now more than ever in an AI-driven world, collaboration is key to navigating complexity and the complex solution spaces analysts work in. With data shared between users, systems, data stores, LLMs, and used by many groups, it is literally impossible to simply analyze it all and the impact of it alone. Analysts and others need to use collaborative analysis models and carefully structured conversation techniques (business analysis techniques) to facilitate getting this work done in a manner that actually meets the needs of the business, users, and customers.

Provide Mentorship and Guidance

Business analysts will need mentors in the following areas to hone the development of various skills:

- Organizational navigation mentors: To help them navigate the complexities of organizations, the various business units and groups they will need to build relationships with, and to understand these groups' goals.

- Leadership mentors: To help analysts develop leadership skills. Someone who can observe their work and provide practical guidance and mentoring in the moment to guide leadership behaviors and development.

- Analysis mentors: To demonstrate and challenge analysts to leverage various analysis techniques and tools.

- Career progression mentors: To help potential analysts and current analysts navigate skills, relationships, and experiences to build a rewarding career within the organization.

Define Clear Expectations

The business analyst's role and job description can differ widely! Many organizations we have worked with have had dozens of job descriptions for this role, and this just does not lead to a clear understanding of the role among teams, leaders, or the organization as a whole. Too many job descriptions focus heavily on the exact knowledge an analyst should have, rather than the skills, mindset, and outcomes they should be able to perform and facilitate. Clearly defined roles, skills, responsibilities, and expected outcomes that are truly about business analysis and facilitating better business outcomes are key.

Inject Regular Feedback

In order to grow and change behaviors, we need feedback, and we need it to be constructive and frequent. Many business analysts have not received this important factor throughout their careers. The ones that have, we have seen grow into amazing professionals! Some analysts in an environment without a strong feedback process have taken it into their own hands and seek it out themselves.

Establishing systems for regular feedback—from leaders, stakeholders, and peers—is a great way to truly help analysts grow. It doesn't have to be complicated. There are simple 360-degree feedback processes, or simple "Start—Stop—Keep" feedback tools to use. The important part is that it happens. Constructive feedback helps analysts refine and reflect on their approach and align better their mindset, the expectations of them, and with the organization's goals.

Infuse Space to Think

Innovative analysis requires time to think. Many analysts complain that between emails, messaging, and meetings there is no time left to think. Encourage yourself, or your team, to block out thinking time and make it a priority. Encourage and highlight where you or other analysts used "time to think" and "collaboration with others" to solve problems and create breakthrough moments for tough problems. Allow analysts the freedom to take time to think, be creative, brainstorm, and collaborate to come up with innovative solutions. This might mean setting up dedicated time, "innovation labs," team space, or simply fostering a culture that values time to think.

Build a Business Analysis Community

Analysts often say they feel lonely at their workplace. They often feel alone in their role, and without others that "get them", without a community to share, learn, and be supported by.

Building a community of practice or a network of analysts within the organization is one way to address this challenge. Regular meetings, knowledge-sharing sessions, focused skill sessions, and fun can foster a sense of shared purpose and growth.

Provide Recognition

Telling success stories is so powerful! Recognize and reward outstanding performance that demonstrates the behaviors and practices you want to see repeated. It's not just about cheering a team that has success, it's about highlighting the behaviors and practices that likely made that success happen for the organizational business results, and what we want to see repeated and modeled by more teams. This storytelling and recognition not only motivates analysts, but it also sets a benchmark of excellence for others to follow, while educating others on what good analysis looks like.

Setting up your organization and business analysts for analysis success is an ongoing commitment. It requires an environment that encourages continuous learning, fosters collaboration, offers the right tools, rewards new skill practice, and, most importantly, values the immense skills, knowledge, and unique contributions that analysts bring to an organization. With the right support structure, analysts can thrive and drive transformative change, immense strategic alignment, facilitate value delivery, and guide organizations toward a brighter, AI-enhanced future.

An Updated View of Business Analysis

In an AI-driven world, business analysis will move closer to business strategy as the details, such as code and designs, are created more and more by AI. The details will be very important, but take less time to work within, and more time will be needed to ensure the context and strategic alignment.

The missing piece for most teams, projects, products, and organizations is linking the strategic intent to the work. With AI, we can now more easily link the strategy to the details, as long as we have analysis skills in place to make the connection.

The key skills and practices of business analysis will be to

- create a well-defined business strategy with measurable customer and user metrics,

- confirm this is in place and help define the measurements if they are not in place,

- connect the metrics to the actual data that will measure them,

- define and connect the value streams and customer journeys to these metrics and data,

- set up ongoing measurements of these key measures and track them ongoing,

- monitor the performance of a value stream and customer journey,

- take the combination of actual evidence of the process performance with the backlog and determine the next priority based on strategic alignment,

- create and define the hypothesis that helps connect the backlog and/or performance measurement issue or discrepancy and what might fix it,

- recommend what gets worked on based on what is most likely to shift the strategic measurements in the right direction,

- define, create, and facilitate **experiments** and small items to prototype and see the measurements' impact,

- define and create the scenarios and tests that need to be covered in the working prototypes, and the corresponding tests with expected results to test them, and

- show stakeholders the results of such prototypes and tests to facilitate decision-making to implement.

This is very different from today's practices that focus on templates, documents, tools, and processes. Being more aligned to strategic intent and strategic measurements is the future as we can more easily link the data for the measurements to the actual products and services.

Chapter Summary

- Many business analysts are not set up for success, for many reasons that the organization, team, managers, or analysts themselves can change.

- There are many ways to strengthen the business analyst's role in the organization, on the team, or on your own.

- An updated view of business analysis in an AI world can help set up organizational analysis success.

Action Items

- Evaluate whether you are set up for success with AI. What factors and challenges are you up against?
- What aspects of strengthening the business analyst's role resonate best with you? Which do not, and why?
- How does this updated view of business analysis or the role change your perception of what success means?

These action items aim to evaluate your readiness for AI as a baseline. A more strategic role is needed with business analysis to enable more success for organizations failing to link strategy to delivery.

9   How to Build These Competencies

Building competency is no small task! It is a process that requires focus and dedication. AI is forcing us to focus on competency and skill development on many levels to survive.

In this chapter we look at what building competency means and the steps to build it in your self or your team and organization. We also discuss the factors that influence building competency.

Vignette

Samantha Ghent

I now also have skill development the way I want it to be. Elise, a junior business analyst, logs into the learning management system (LMS), and it runs in the background. Through settings within the LMS, Elise has allowed it to track her work and recommend learning. An AI-driven interface greets her: "Good morning, Elise. Based on your recent initiative, your meeting schedule, and your emails and messaging content, here are some recommended mini-courses for today." The courses range from advanced data visualization techniques to the psychology of team dynamics, each tailored to Elise's current needs and future career aspirations. Elise can ask the LMS questions about her upcoming meetings today and in the next week, and get coaching responses and five-minute learning recommendations to help her prepare. The LMS also recommends mentors in her organization who have mastered these skills, and it offers to set up a coffee chat with them.

Building Competency is a Continuous Journey

In order to learn how to build a skill, we need to look at how skills are developed. We know that business analysis is a complex skillset—a knowledge worker skillset—and these skills take years to build competency in. So, to build skills at a high level, we need to not just gain knowledge about the skill, but practice it, reflect and/or get feedback on it, then learn more, practice more, perform it in different contexts, and continue to learn and reflect.

In the past, some business analysts could "get by" without specific analysis skills and could use their domain knowledge or hide behind others who dictated solutions, never really knowing whether their work made an impact. This will no longer work, and the value of this approach will be questioned; the knowledge in the organization can be readily accessed by anyone with organizational, operational, systems, and external knowledge, accessible through GenAI with LLMs.

The actual business analysis skillset is what will set organizations apart as it becomes the critical path to creating change. Those operating without these deep analysis skills will no longer be able to hide behind the curtain of knowledge. Knowledge will be too easily accessed with AI. Experience and judgment will be valued, and it is with analysis skills that the magic lies.

In the future, learning for business analysts and knowledge workers will become a fluid blend of structured daily mini-bites, mini-courses, mentoring, real-time information, immersive experiences, and practical applications. AI enables learning to be deeply personal, highly relevant, and immensely efficient, ensuring that these professionals are always at the forefront of their fields and growing as they are ready and empowered to do.

Business analysis is a skill constantly rated as one of the most in-demand. It's not just the title, rather due to how many titles, roles, and professionals need these skills for organizations.

Organizations and leaders are aware that business analysis skills are important, yet those who fail to actually invest specifically in the skill or the roles that depend on this skill success lag behind.

In an AI-driven world, the importance of business analysis at all levels, from strategic to implementation, will become more of a differentiator. The key business analysis activities in organizations will do the following:

- Determine what initiative to invest in, and how much it is worth investing, based on
  - strategic alignment, not the person who shouts the loudest,
  - aligned data and metrics, not siloed metrics or none at all, and
  - consensus of leaders that they are willing to support a hypothesis, rather than strong opinions.

- Monitor process, customer journey, and value stream performance, through
  - defining and setting up the metrics that matter to strategically align,
  - understanding when to address a variance, and
  - investigating and recommending solutions.

- Prioritize ideas, defects, variances, and enhancements to implement, through
  - analyzing the backlog as a holistic view of potential things that may increase process performance and value, and
  - defining and prioritizing which **hypotheses and experiments** to run.

- Define and prioritize incremental improvements on these that test our assumptions of what is valuable as we build and spend, also allowing for changing circumstances.

- Create a shared understanding of options and alternatives for decision-making, by
  - identifying and communicating the various options and alternatives, and
  - facilitating the group to a decision.

- Facilitate the details of the option selected to move forward by
  - creating or updating the **assets**, including
    - user scenarios and expected results at different levels of detail,
    - user—process—data—rules structured information, at different levels of detail,
    - acceptance criteria: running the test to see if it meets acceptance, at different levels of detail,
    - checking roles are current within the **assets** of who is accountable,
    - validating all locational information across global sites, and
    - ensuring all temporal timings across **assets** are valid.

- Facilitate the build and testing process for an incremental improvement through
  - testing, tracking, and collaborating with others to get to test results to make a decision on whether to deploy, and
  - updating the monitoring of the solution based on deployed changes.

What Does Building Competency Mean?

Building competencies in any skill, for yourself or a group, can be a daunting task. It requires focus, dedication, and a plan.

Angela's Story

> When I learned how to ride a bike, I was about four years old. I remember watching my older brother and neighbor kids ride, and this motivated me to learn. I might say I was analyzing them to plan my quest of learning to ride, but the analysis I was able to do was pretty limited.
>
> Instead of watching and analyzing, at some point I knew I just had to build the courage to try! I remember two trees in our front yard, about 40 feet apart, and I attempted to ride from one tree to the other. I fell, I wobbled, and sometimes I prevailed. I kept learning, getting better and better at it, eventually consistently making it all the way to the next tree, then around them in circles, and eventually out onto the street. As riding got more complex (in the street), I encountered slopes; some I saw, some I did not! I had to learn what this meant and how to handle it. Parked cars and curbs were other obstacles, and of course moving things, like people and cars. The skill I thought I had perfected of riding a bike kept getting more complex with the context and environment as I strayed further from the isolated front yard.
>
> I had to learn in phases, but phases of value iterations where I learned by increasing the context and complexity.
>
> Solving problems, building software, and user experiences are similar. We can't analyze it all upfront. And, with increasing complexity, we will fail with upfront analysis as an approach. Just like learning to ride a bike "out in the wild," the context, environment, and complexity changes.We just have to start learning, accelerate the learning process while analyzing along the way; and, as the situation changes, we must respond to the change. Analyzing the focus on the goals we have.
>
> My goal was to be able to ride to my friend's house and to the park. I couldn't just take a class, I had to practice, reflect, fail, get feedback and coaching, and increase the complexity of the skill as I learned. I had to demonstrate to myself and my parents that I could handle the various obstacles and risks to making what was a valuable journey to me.

How to Build These Competencies

It's not just about attending a training class. Courses are about acquiring knowledge, but this is just the first step of many to build competency. It is about going from knowledge to comprehension; understanding the knowledge, then applying and using the knowledge, then tying other concepts together and analyzing, synthesizing, and evaluating to make good judgments, as depicted in the following diagram.

When it comes to professional knowledge and worker skill development, this process takes application and practice to gain experience, not just courses. It takes experience, failing, learning from others, and applying the skill in various contexts.

We can gain knowledge from a course, but the learner's previous experience and context impacts how they take the knowledge into their realm of comprehension. No two people will take the same learning and understand it in exactly the same way, due to their various contexts of understanding and their previous experiences. Once we have the knowledge and have assimilated it to our own context and experiences, we begin to comprehend it at a level as deep as we connect it to that context. This means that no two people will understand the same course in the same way or at the same level of depth.

We can ask ourselves and our teams to use new skills, but many will not have the support needed to practice them and will revert to previous ways of working. Once we are supported to try, fail, and practice, then skill development moves forward.

We have found that about 10% of people will try without a strong support structure, but the majority will not. It is up to each individual or organization to understand this and develop strategies to get the support needed.

Support to learn new skills comes through

- the manager, leader, or peer coaching and mentoring,

- seeing other peers and leaders demonstrate the skill,

- being supported through trying and failing,

- external mentoring and coaching,

- stakeholder management where the recipients of the new skill are talked to and expectations are set and established,

- proactive time to learn, try, reflect, and get feedback, and

- permission to fail and learn from failing.

Building business analysis skills and competencies is about so much more than simply buying a course. This applies to many things we can relate to in life: learning to cook, driving, photography skills, learning another language. The courses and knowledge are just the first step.

Even when we have years of experience, we may not have ever learned the true skills and techniques needed to succeed. How many of us have cooked or taken photos for years, yet have never had formal training to understand the key practices to do it really well in different contexts and complexities? Once we have the training, we still need to assimilate it and see ourselves doing it, find the motivation to practice, see the results, and practice/adjust some more! The powerful combination of experience, courses/knowledge, and mentoring is not any different in business analysis.

Steps to Building Competency

The overall steps to build competency are to first assess where you are at—current state. Then, identify the skill gaps, set goals and prioritize them, plan and implement a skills plan, then monitor, track, and support it. Adjust as you learn what is working, and then reassess to see progress.

This process may seem daunting and like a lot of work. But, not upskilling may cause more pain! The skills needed for any role are changing fast, and business analysis is no different.

Changing skills in any team impacts them and any other roles they interact with. A huge part of the success of building competencies and growing is working with the other roles who will experience different skills and techniques that are being used as input to their work. This aspect of building business analysis competency is often neglected.

If you are working alone to upskill, make sure you think through who you work with and what matters to them. Even when we are using poor practices, our stakeholders and teammates are often still quite comfortable with them. So, changing processes on them, even to perform better analysis, may feel strange and even threatening if they depend on and expect the old ways of working. It takes a bit of finesse to help others understand and accept the changes we make in our skills, techniques, and practices to get better analysis done.

Changing analysis practices without due care as to who uses our work can be a difficult situation to find ourselves in.

Upskilling business analysis skills is vital in the rapidly changing business and technology environment. A structured skill-building process can ensure that you or your team remain competitive and can meet the evolving demands and skills needed to successfully perform high-quality business analysis.

Here are some things to consider when working on you, or your team/organization's skill-building process.

1. Perform a skill gap analysis/assessment to determine
   - desired outcomes—what you want your practice to look like,
   - current skills inventory—assess the current skills against a catalog of desired skills, and
   - gaps—compare the current inventory with desired outcomes to pinpoint areas of improvement.
2. Prioritize skills to ask
   - Which skills are immediately needed?
   - Which can be developed over a longer time?
   - Which skills will take more time, due to not having any internal mentors and coaches?
   - Which will be more difficult due to culture and possible behavior changes in others?
3. Then select the learning approach, such as
   - in-person training,
   - online courses,
   - online skill memberships with on-demand and live events, with instructor interaction,
   - industry trade association membership,
   - workshops and seminars, for hands-on experience or deeper dives into subjects,
   - webinars, which are useful for remote teams or bringing in external experts,
   - peer-to-peer learning, which encourages knowledge sharing among professionals, and
   - conferences.
4. In corporate practice and experiential learning through
   - on-the-job training, which allows professionals to apply new skills in real-world scenarios, and consider who the trainers, mentors, and coaches will be,
   - mentorship programs where you pair less-skilled professionals with experienced mentors, and
   - job rotation, where you expose professionals to different roles or departments to broaden skillsets.

How to Build These Competencies

5. Monitor progress and adapt as necessary through
    -   measuring not just the course completion checkmarks, but the next steps of competency development (practicing, feedback, mentoring, etc.),
    -   creating a feedback system where professionals can escalate when a certain point is not working for them (is the learning not effective? Do they not have the opportunity to practice? Is the support and mentoring lacking?). Make sure the feedback hits all the stages of skill development, not just the first step of acquiring the knowledge, and
    -   being ready to modify the approach and plan, and adjust.
6. Evaluate outcomes to
    -   reassess skills and compare—assessment should be about more than learning, but also the practice and progress of competency development overall,
    -   see how professionals apply new skills in their roles, tell the stories, and understand the practicality of what they are experiencing, and
    -   gain feedback from others—collect input from stakeholders about how new skills are working.
7. Reinforce learning through
    -   offering periodic refresher sessions to ensure retention of skills,
    -   fostering an environment where ongoing learning is valued and encouraged, and
    -   acknowledging and rewarding professionals who show significant skill improvement.
8. Integrate with career development by
    -   showing how these new skills can contribute to various career paths, and
    -   identifying potential leaders for succession planning, and ensure they're gaining the skills needed for higher roles.
9. Facilitate continuous improvement through
    -   staying updated—as industries evolve, update the skills training to match,
    -   seeking external insights by bringing in industry experts or consultants to provide fresh perspectives on skill building, and
    -   reviewing and refining the entire skill-building process periodically and making adjustments as needed.

A successful skill-building process is iterative and should be adapted based on feedback, outcomes, and changing needs and goals. Staying relevant in a fast-paced and ever-evolving world requires leaders to be proactive and intentional about their own learning, as well as facilitating learning for their teams.

Factors Influencing Competency Development

Internal Mobility as a Key Competency Development Driver

Internal mobility, coupled with skills development, is rapidly emerging as a cornerstone strategy for organizations looking to remain agile and innovative in the face of change. Let's explore how internal mobility and skills act as drivers for organizations and individuals to build future-ready capabilities.

From an organizational perspective, four things are important to skills development for business analysts:

- Business agility: As businesses pivot or adapt to market changes and internal mobility, the competency uplift ensures they can quickly reallocate talent to where it's most needed, without the time and expense of external hiring processes.

- Cost savings: Internal hiring and transfers are generally more cost effective than recruiting from the outside. The organization already has a sense of the employee's work ethic, culture fit, and potential.

- Retention: Offering opportunities for lateral or upward movement within the organization can significantly increase employee satisfaction and retention. This counters the high costs associated with turnover and knowledge loss.

- Knowledge continuity: Internal mobility allows for better preservation and transfer of institutional knowledge. As employees move into new roles, they bring with them knowledge of other departments or initiatives, fostering cross-functional collaboration. A focus on value streams and customer journeys is key for knowledge continuity because these **assets** change at a slower pace than software functions and technology.

From an individual perspective, there are also strong considerations for why skill development and internal mobility are important, such as the following:

- Career growth: You are not confined to a fixed career path and have the opportunity to explore various roles, skills, and areas of an organization.

- Personal development: By gaining experience in multiple roles and skills, you will acquire a broader perspective and a diverse skillset, making you even more versatile and valuable.

- Motivation: Knowing that the organization values your growth and offers pathways for internal mobility can significantly boost your loyalty and motivation.

- Relevance: Continuous skills development ensures that you remain relevant in today's changing landscape.

How to Build These Competencies

Skill development from an individual and organizational perspective can also bring about some great benefits, such as the following:

- Future readiness: By focusing on continuous skills development, organizations ensure they have the talent pool ready to address future challenges and capitalize on new opportunities.

- Cultural shift: A culture that emphasizes learning and development is more adaptable to change, is innovative, and better equipped to face uncertainties.

- Productivity and innovation: Skilled employees can drive efficiencies, improve processes, and contribute innovative solutions.

As the future of work evolves, individuals and organizations that prioritize business analysis skills as a key strategy to their internal mobility and continuous skills development will position themselves, and their teams, for continued success. Such organizations are not just reacting to change but are proactively shaping their futures through innovation.

What to Focus on First—A Roadmap to Get There

| Assets | Hypothesis and Experiments | Team Tasks and Activities | Deliverables | User Behavior Changes | Business Results |

For some organizations, the **AI Analysis Accelerator Framework**, skills, and even role of analysis and a business analyst may be far from where you or your organization are currently at. For other organizations and individuals, this is a welcome and articulated framework of what "just makes sense" and what is intuitively needed. And, of course, many will be somewhere in-between.

Here is a pathway that we hope will help guide your learning and practice development to bring an AI and analysis framework together and your organization into the future.

The most important practice that we recommend starting with is metrics.

Define Metrics

Start defining the metrics that matter and link the analysis work to them. This involves the following steps:

1. For each initiative, project, feature, epic (or whatever you are using), define the user behavior changes that would make it successful. Link these to the work being done, the strategic intent, and the higher-level objectives the team is working on.
2. Start questioning and looking at how you are defining "projects" and "teams." Are they aligned to these user behaviors or siloed from them? Just observe for now.
3. Define and understand what data will measure these user behavior changes, and start tracking it. Track it while developing, and then keep tracking it after. Make an analyst responsible for tracking this and analyzing when and why it is moving.
4. Start using the metrics definitions and actual data in project kick-off, update, status meetings, sprint reviews, demos, release updates, etc. Start building a culture and habit of using this data and measuring this to discuss success.
5. Start looking at the backlog holistically toward these metrics. Can you align each item to the user behaviors they support? If so, to what part of the workflow and smaller user action that the item enables?
6. When looking at the process and user performance data, what would you add to the backlog? Would you prioritize it higher than other items and why? Start having these conversations with leaders.
7. Start experimenting with putting this process performance data into an AI tool to analyze it. Ask what recommendations it has.

This change to your analysis practices alone will drive major change and immediately give you a lift in results.

Key to implementing this is to find a meaningful place to use it and make it visible to everyone and a natural part of the conversations, i.e., a place that will enable this to be part of every conversation the team has all the time. Perhaps it becomes your epic level, and then you can trace up and down to the user stories and requirements that align to making this user behavior happen.

For example, if the medical appointment booking project has an API team working on the API between the web service and the calendaring system, this team is still linked to the user behavior change of booking appointments online. Yes, these technical details can make or break the user behavior, and without this team thinking about it, they are not likely to ask the right questions, test the right scenarios, and collaborate effectively to link their work to the correct front and backend details.

Build Assets

Start building **assets** for reuse and a culture of **assets** as reference for the team, rather than these being **deliverables**.

Start with a customer journey map for one project. Identify who your customers are, what their needs are, and what path they will take in getting their needs met. With a customer journey map there are a few key pieces not to miss. Many get confused about what a customer journey map is and what makes them different from a process model, but what is really important here is the emotions component, and the scope of the model being far wider than the system itself.

People do not necessarily want to use your product or system, they are often forced to, or they choose to use it because it helps them get something done; they want the system to make this task easier than the alternative.

Remember our medical appointment booking example? No patient wants to have to go through the steps to make an appointment. They want to see a doctor and not be in pain, or they want to prevent illness. Making an appointment years ago was 100% done by phone call, or at the reception desk at the doctor's office. Phone calls are often painful to schedule, with multiple holds, transfers, and an often-lengthy conversation back and forth about dates and times. The customer's journey is about the emotion of hearing they have to make another appointment, rearrange their schedule, take time off work, arrange transportation, etc. This is not a fun task to take on! Neither is using a system that is not any easier.

Personally, we have experienced a few online scheduling systems in the medical domain, and we have given up—it is easier to call. Scary! We are sure that these systems were a nice project that was scoped out, estimated, and then designed, built, and tested on schedule and on budget. So, why didn't they work?

Because the customer journey wasn't taken into consideration. If the analysis had been done and the key metrics were tracked, these solutions would have never made it far into production and caused users so much pain. What was the pain?

Context first: We might typically find out about the online scheduling system by calling to make an appointment, and while on hold waiting for a scheduler, we would hear a lovely message saying, "Want to get off hold? Book online! Go to www.abcdefg.com to schedule your appointment now!" *Okay, wonderful*, we might think, and go to the website. We then need to set up an account or retrieve a forgotten password. A serious pain, especially when we just lost our place on hold, and now we are delayed with this! But, alas, this is a somewhat normal thing. We begrudgingly go through the motions in the hope of a speedy appointment setup. Coming into this new scheduling feature, we are already aggravated, but full of hope! The pain was just beginning. The first step was to select a clinician. Simple enough, and logical. Then, we are supposed to select an appointment type (a bit confusing, as surely "seeing a doctor" is the goal; as patients, we don't analyze the types of appointments). Next, we need to select a date. At first glance we think, *Wonderful, we can choose a date!* Then, *This is odd, typically it's pretty hard to find a date, and the dates are booked out several weeks or months, with only a few isolated appointments close up.*

After selecting a date, we are asked to select a time of day. Again, a bit of mixed emotions between excitement and confusion. After selecting a time, we are asked to "submit." Then a little hourglass image shows while we wait to see the appointment confirmation. But, instead, we get a message that the combination of doctor, appointment type, date, and time is not available. Ugh! We try a few more times as the system asks us to start over, and then, with complete frustration, think, *I am not sure I will ever be successful with this! Why can't the system just tell me what IS available?* So, frustrated, we give up and call to make an appointment.

Two key questions, therefore, are:

- What aspects of the customer journey have what emotions?
- What does the bigger picture tell us?

A customer journey map would map this all out, show the painful parts of the process before the user even gets to the scheduling system, and then play out these common scenarios more. In turn, when used by a business analyst in collaboration with key user behavior metrics, stakeholders, data analytics, and the dev team, the team would have likely designed something very different.

Other **assets** that can be built along the way include

- value streams,

- business capability hierarchy,

- data mapped to processes,

- defined user groups,

- defined business rules,

- state transition diagrams/tables,

- dataflow diagrams, and

- revenue and expense impact models.

Remember that these **assets** are not a phase, nor a deliverable; they are ongoing **assets** that are created, used, and updated through good business analysis practice. Reusing **assets** helps business agility through fast impact assessments.

Think about when you are doing some updates to your house and each project has a phase that would recreate the blueprints, electrical map, plumbing schema, etc. Ugh!

Angela's Story

This happened to me recently where one of my master bedroom outlets kept trapping a circuit when I would use my hairdryer. I would need to go to the fuse box and flip the circuit to get the lights and electrics back on in that part of the house. Eventually, I got annoyed enough to call an electrician. Before they arrived, I realized that my circuit box was not documented and mapped to the outlets. This is an asset that would be extremely helpful to solve and fix the problem. And, it was very expensive to have someone map out for me before they could even get to work on the real issue at hand.

Ideally, the circuit box would have had the "asset" of the mappings, and it would be updated regularly and used by any other electrical worker over the last 50 years for the house. Without it, I do not have any agility to fix and update anything.

Tim's Story

In the fast-paced world of the entertainment industry, I had the opportunity to work as a consultant for a company that was undertaking a massive multi-year program of work. The objective was to develop software that would support the organization's revenue and expense drivers across the value chain.

With a strategic mindset, my team and I carefully mapped out the value chain, ensuring that each process asset was connected back to the core drivers of the business. It wa s a challenging but rewarding endeavor, as we delved into various projects, linking processes, and establishing a hierarchy that drilled down to the required detail level to implement business rules and data.

As the program unfolded over the years, we didn't just document processes, we identified key metrics showcasing the benefits each process brought to the organization. We left no stone unturned, tracing the intricacies of who managed, performed, and received process information. We validated the geographical locations of each process and meticulously understood any unique temporal timing implications.

By the end of the multi-year change initiative, I had not just captured and documented these **assets**, but had baselined them, creating a robust foundation architecture for future endeavors to build upon.

One day, a particularly astute executive, having thoroughly examined the asset creation, approached me in the car park. A grin spread across their face as they expressed, "I now fully understand the business across all departments." However, what came next caught me off guard with sheer joy: "We could now lift and shift our business overseas."

I and my team helped them shift the business overseas, to other parts of Australia, and expand their products using reusable architecture **assets**.

In the end, it wasn't just about understanding the business; it was about enabling its evolution and growth on a scale that surpassed even my initial ambitions.

How to Build These Competencies

Can AI Help Create and Maintain These Assets?

Yes. AI can help us create many of these **assets** for business analysis. The question is, is your team using AI for this purpose, and do they have enough experience, judgment, and business analysis skill to know how to leverage AI to help create many of the **assets** needed?

AI has the ability to create most, if not all, of the models business analysts use. AI can create them from text descriptions, from reading code, and from other creative prompting. So, while in the past analysts learned how to create these models, now they need to know when to use them, the prompt to create them, interpret them, analyze them, and edit or update them (or tell an AI assistant what to update).

Once you have these **assets** in place, and an accountability to create, manage, update from "as is" to "to be" continuously, and use them appropriately in your practice, the next step is to map data to them. Yes, real production data.

Monitor and Evaluate Value Stream and Customer Journey Performance

The real magic of AI is taking various AI capabilities and using them together. For example:

- using robotics with GenAI such that humans can chat with robots,

- using data analytics, deep learning, and GenAI such that we can ask and chat with AI assistants about the data, patterns, and predictions, and

- using visual AI recognition with GenAI and data analytics to predict things based on images, video, etc.

With your key metrics of **user behaviors** identified, and with your **assets** mapped to data, you will be ready to take advantage of leveraging AI in many capacities. This will dramatically increase the agility in the organization and enable the proactive nature of addressing challenges before customers and business leaders even know there is a problem.

Steps to get started:

1. Set up a dashboard environment and an owner for a value stream.
2. Set up the dashboard analysis to measure and monitor the key performance user metrics.
3. Have a business analyst own the analysis process, analyze variations in the data, discuss with business owners, and use it as input to add to the backlog and analyze backlog priorities.

Angela's Story

I was on a project team that fell into this by accident. We had implemented a large system for a call center, and with tight deadlines we went into day one with an already long list of items on the backlog, such as things that didn't quite make it into scope, known defects from testing, new requirements that came up during the project that we could not fit in, and more. A few weeks after implementing, I was chatting with some project colleagues and we were observing what we thought were "funny" calls that customers were having with agents. Part of the new project implementation was software that allowed us to watch and eavesdrop on the real production calls, as well as previous calls that had been recorded. While I tried to laugh with everyone at the customer/agent humor, my analytical and serious side was dying for another reason. I was so focused on the user interactions I was seeing that could have been designed and implemented differently, and fixing them would solve some of the leadership's metrics issues.

Before this impromptu "observation" session, I had been in a meeting where leadership was reporting on their business metrics since the new system implementation. The metrics were not yet turning around in the favorable direction that was anticipated. Calls were still taking too long, too many calls were getting transferred due to the wrong type of agent getting the call, and queue times were not shortened. Translate this into user metrics and we get customers on calls longer, customers getting transferred more than they should be, and customers waiting in queue longer than they should be.

I immediately thought that what I saw in the observation session could be easily fixed and turn these metrics around, and fast. I took some quick notes about what I was seeing. Next, I went to look at the ever-growing backlog and didn't see any of these things! No one had reported these issues or put forward improvement ideas.

I felt so strongly about what I was seeing that I quickly contacted my colleague on the data team and found a way to gain his interest in what I was seeing. We worked together to run some quick data reports and analysis and found that what I saw was not an anomaly.

I set up some time with the leadership team the next day, stating to them that I was listening to the leadership update and was concerned about their metrics, and that I had some evidence and ideas to improve it. They were ready to listen since I connected to their metrics! I quickly worked with a dev team lead—less than an hour of their time—to get a relative estimate to fix a few things.

How to Build These Competencies

I presented my findings and ideas to leadership the next day. In the meeting I also presented that nothing on the backlog currently would likely move the metrics like these fixes would, and they agreed. I got approval to immediately stop all current work items, work on these fixes, and pause the backlog we were currently working on. Within 48 hours the fixes were implemented, and I observed and ran the same data I had a few days earlier. The metrics were headed in the right direction.

I share this story because of the powerful message of having business analysis look at metrics, track them, and focus on them. This was all before AI could help, and I was lucky to be able to nimbly get help from various roles to make all this happen. Some were from relationships I had built, some success was my communication skills, some of my critical thinking was used as well; but mostly, it was a mindset. A mindset of my role being to chase metrics that matter. A mindset to not let a predefined backlog run my work order. A mindset that acknowledges that what leaders ask for (in the backlog) doesn't mean it is what will get them the success they need.

With AI today, we can now set up and monitor user process and performance like never before. This type of mindset becomes easier, faster, and more realistic to implement compared to years past.

Talk About Setting Expectations and Stakeholder Change Management of New Practices

One of the biggest challenges in introducing new practices is actually getting ourselves (or the practitioners on your team) to use the new skills, and their stakeholders to accept the change.

The resistance is real, and so is the fear of missing the expectations of stakeholders. Our work in business analysis is usually the middle of a workstream for others. Our work is used as inputs to others. This means that changing our work impacts others. This dynamic makes it incredibly difficult to implement new practices, even when we know the old ones are not serving us or the stakeholders well.

As we change our practices in how we collaborate—the inputs and **assets** we use to collaborate, and the **deliverables** we create as inputs to others' work—we need to address some key considerations:

- Do your stakeholder analysis!

- Who uses your **deliverables**?

- How are they using them?

- What pain points and challenges do they have with their work?

- How do the old/current practices contribute to these challenges?

- How do your new (and better) practices help them do their job better?

Be prepared to have these conversations, and many of them! We recommend one-on-one conversations with key stakeholders and getting them to help you communicate the message to the larger group. In addition, try the following:

- Be willing to set up **experiments** with stakeholders to try out a new process and practice. Make sure to define your **hypothesis** and understand what you are trying to learn from the experiment.

- Assert your expertise! If someone doesn't think it will work, don't abandon a known good practice. Listen to them, take the information they have given you, and go back to the drawing board for other ways to incorporate good practice along with their needs.

We have seen far too many business analysis teams abandon good practices due to one stakeholder saying they don't like it.

For example, when a developer is insisting on analysts providing technical details or specs. Recognize that this is not a good business analysis practice, and does not lead to good technical practices either. An analyst should provide good practice requirements that are without the technical level of detail, allowing the technically skilled team members to use their technical expertise to make those decisions.

The analyst may have some important knowledge that helps the technical team solve the technical details, and this should not be ignored. This knowledge should come out in the collaboration between the analyst and technical team, not as part of requirements handed off. A collaboration with the technical roadmap and standards along with the business and user needs is what makes the difference.

When a developer continues to push for technical details, we need to seek to understand what the issue is for them. It could be that they do not have the skills to do software engineering and are measured by how fast they code. This then is a bigger issue that cannot be solved by the developer, but rather leadership higher up. In this case, it's another stakeholder we need to influence and get support from. How can not giving the developer the technical level of detail they ask for improve their development practices? What role in their team/organization can be brought into the conversation to help fill in this gap?

Having analysts write requirements with technical details simply creates technical debt, poorly architected systems, and does not allow for a technical roadmap and best practices to be implemented.

High-quality business analysis is key to organizational business agility, and poor practices will no longer be tolerated. It is critical that **assets** be continually updated, which is possible with AI.

Organisations with a strong business architecture foundation will be better positioned to respond to market pressures as the flexibility of fast **hypotheses and experiments** using AI and predictive data that measure **user behavior changes** will make continuous improvements possible and highly accurate.

Chapter Summary

- The concept of business analysis is not changing; however, the mindset, skills, actions, and what it looks and feels like for analysts and their stakeholders is changing greatly.

- Building new competencies is a process and not just about training and acquiring knowledge. It takes a lot more to develop the skills needed to thrive and bring out the expected value of business analysis.

- Your roadmap to create these competencies may look different than before, yet the basics of metrics, stakeholder analysis, and change management still prevail.

Action Items

- Assess how your business analyst role/practice/discipline aligns with the key activities listed in this chapter. Does your role align? Who does these things if analysts do not?
- How does your current competency development process empower the steps mentioned in this chapter? What is missing or needs improving?
- Start creating your roadmap to developing new competencies ready for an AI-immersed world!

These action items aim to help you align your role to success. Competency development must be continuous, and futureproofing through learning will be the key, so start today with creating a roadmap.

10 Last Words from Samantha Ghent

As time passes, I reflect on this journey. I am pleased with choosing the path of integrating business analysis creatively and effectively along with our AI-first strategy. The organization has become adept at identifying and solving complex business problems, and the organization is flourishing in unexpected ways.

These are some key lessons that I learned and reflect on often, and remind others about often:

- *Understanding over automation: We must understand the "why" behind the work and align to it.*
- *The human element: We learned that the best business analysis always considers the human impact. "A process that doesn't make life easier for people is like a screen door on a submarine," was a favorite analogy.*
- *Collaboration is key: We found that involving diverse teams in analysis led to innovative solutions.*
- *Data quality over quantity: More data doesn't necessarily mean better insights. "It's like having a closet full of clothes but nothing to wear," we would joke.*
- *The importance of a skilled team: My leadership team and I realized that AI is only as good as the team behind it.*

As months turned into years, I am glad we took this path by implementing AI and business analysis in a way that was both effective and enjoyable. The team has grown more confident and skilled, and the business is thriving in ways we never imagined.

But perhaps the most amusing outcome was the AI-powered coffee machine I installed, which predicted the type of coffee each employee needed based on their morning mood. It was a hit, except for the time it offered the CFO a decaf just before a crucial meeting with shareholders!

www.ingramcontent.com/pod-product-compliance
Lightning Source LLC
Chambersburg PA
CBHW080554060326
40689CB00021B/4848